Moving Average Mastery: Proven Strategies for Perfect Entry & Exit Timing

Unlock Proven Trade Signals Using the Most Reliable Trend Indicator in the Market

By Grant Westbrook

First Edition

Table of Contents

Introduction

Whether you're a novice looking to understand the basics of day trading or an experienced trader seeking to refine your strategy, this book will provide you with the knowledge and tools to master one of the most powerful and widely used indicators in technical analysis: the **Moving Average**.

In the world of day trading and futures trading, the ability to identify trends, manage risk, and time entries and exits effectively can make the difference between consistent profits and costly mistakes. The moving average is a cornerstone of technical analysis, helping traders smooth out price fluctuations and spot clear trends in a noisy market. Whether you trade oil, gold, or stock index futures, moving averages offer a tried-and-true method for understanding market behavior and improving your trading decisions.

Throughout this guide, you'll learn the theory behind moving averages, how they're calculated, and the various types of moving averages used by traders today. You'll explore how to use moving averages to spot trends, confirm entry and exit points, and manage risk in your trades. We'll also delve into advanced strategies, combining moving averages with other technical tools to enhance your decision-making and increase the odds of success in your trading journey.

In this book, you will find:

- **A clear breakdown of moving averages**, including how to calculate and interpret them, so that you can apply them to your trades with confidence.

- **Step-by-step guides** to understanding the different types of moving averages—such as Simple Moving Averages (SMA) and Exponential Moving Averages (EMA)—and when to use each one.

- **Practical strategies** for using moving averages to enter and exit trades effectively, whether you're day trading, swing trading, or investing for the long term.

- **Real-world examples** showing how moving averages are used in real market scenarios across different timeframes and markets, including futures, stocks, and commodities.

- **Tips on managing risk** by using moving averages as dynamic support and resistance levels, as well as how to use them in conjunction with other technical indicators for more accurate trade signals.

In addition to the technical aspects, you'll also gain insight into the psychology of trading—how to trust your moving average signals and avoid common pitfalls such as overtrading and chasing the market. Understanding how moving averages can fit into your overall trading plan will be key to achieving long-term success.

By the end of this book, you'll have the knowledge to confidently integrate moving averages into your trading strategies, enhancing your ability to read the market and make informed decisions.

Are you ready to take your trading to the next level and unlock the potential of one of the most effective trend-following tools in technical analysis? Let's dive in

Chapter 1

Understanding Moving Averages

What is a Moving Average?

A **Moving Average (MA)** is one of the most important and widely used technical indicators in day trading and financial analysis. It is an essential tool that helps traders smooth out past price data to identify trends, potential reversal points, and areas of support and resistance. In essence, a moving average helps traders and investors make sense of the fluctuating prices in the market by simplifying price action.

The moving average is called "moving" because it is constantly updated, incorporating the most recent prices into its calculation and dropping the oldest data points. This dynamic nature helps traders to gauge the overall direction of a market and adapt to changing market conditions.

At its core, a moving average takes a set period of price data (such as the last 10, 50, or 200 periods) and calculates the average for that timeframe. As new price data becomes available, the oldest data is dropped, and a new average is calculated. This smoothing process helps eliminate short-term price fluctuations and highlights the underlying trend in the market, whether it's an uptrend, downtrend, or sideways movement.

Key Characteristics of a Moving Average:

- **Price Smoothing**: Moving averages filter out the "noise" created by short-term price fluctuations, making it easier to see the prevailing trend. This smoothing effect can help traders stay focused on the broader market movement instead of being distracted by daily price swings.

- **Trend-Following Tool**: Moving averages are primarily used to identify and confirm the trend. Since they are lagging indicators (they rely on past prices), they reflect what has already happened in the market, but they do so in a way that helps traders make more informed decisions.
    - When the price is consistently above a moving average, it is generally considered an uptrend.

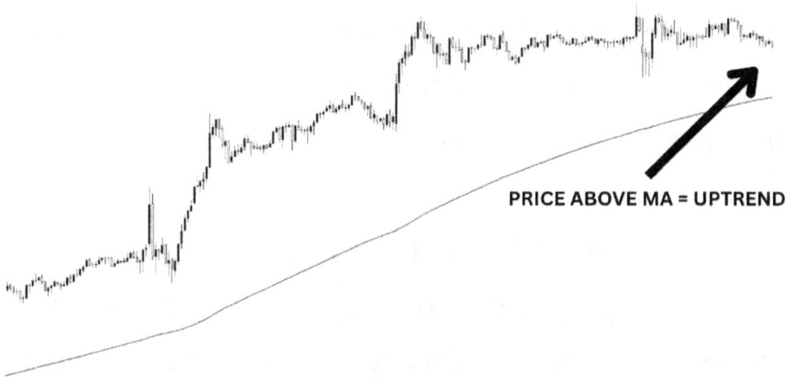

- ◦ When the price is consistently below, it suggests a downtrend.

- **Lagging Indicator**: It's important to note that moving averages are lagging indicators. This means they don't predict future prices but rather help confirm the direction that the market has already started moving in. Although they may not provide early entry points, they help avoid getting caught in false breakouts or "whipsaws" by confirming trends after they are already in motion.

- **Trend Reversals and Crossovers**: One of the most powerful applications of moving averages is spotting trend reversals. Traders commonly use a **crossover strategy**, where a shorter-term moving average crosses over a longer-term moving average.

- For example, when the 10-period moving average crosses above the 50-period moving average, it can signal a bullish trend.

- Conversely, when a shorter-term moving average crosses below a longer-term moving average, it may signal a bearish trend.

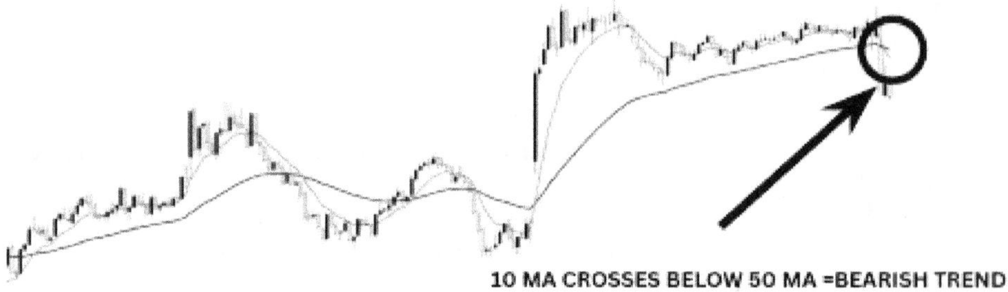

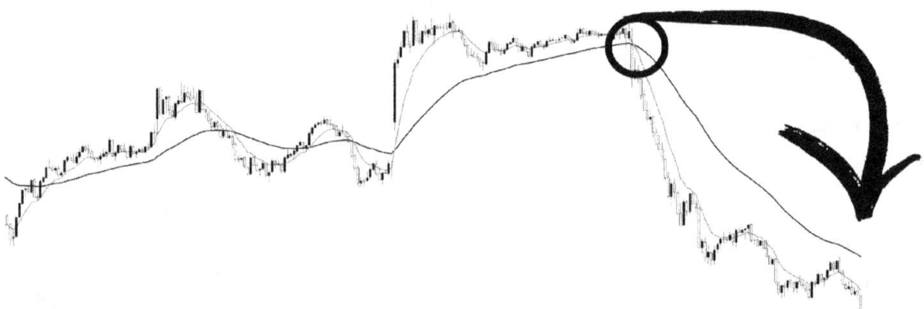

- **Support and Resistance Levels**: Moving averages can also act as dynamic levels of support or resistance.
    - In an uptrend, a moving average may serve as support when the price pulls back.

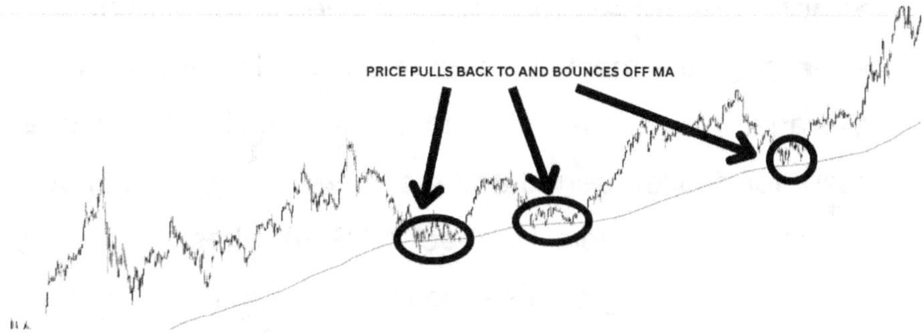

    - In a downtrend, it can act as resistance during retracements.

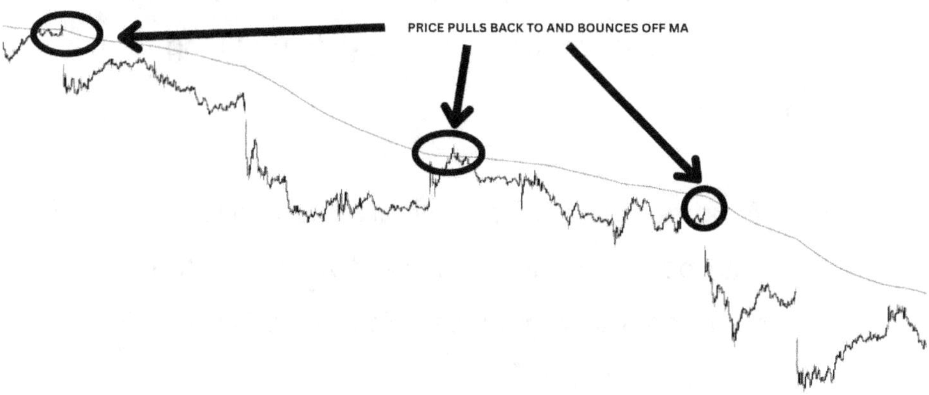

    - Traders often use this behavior to set stop-loss orders or target price levels.

Types of Moving Averages

There are several types of moving averages, but the two most common are:

1. **Simple Moving Average (SMA)**: The **Simple Moving Average** is the most basic and traditional type of moving average. It is calculated by adding the closing prices of an asset for a given period and then dividing by the number of periods. For example, a 10-period SMA takes the average of the last 10 closing prices. The result is a smooth line that reflects the average price over the chosen timeframe.

    - **Strengths**: The SMA is easy to calculate and understand, making it ideal for beginners. It is effective at identifying the direction of long-term trends.

    - **Weaknesses**: Because it gives equal weight to all data points, it can be slower to respond to rapid price changes, making it less effective in fast-moving or volatile markets.

2. **Exponential Moving Average (EMA)**: The **Exponential Moving Average** places more weight on the most recent price data, making it more responsive to recent price movements. Unlike the SMA, the EMA is calculated by giving a greater weight to the latest prices, which means it reacts more quickly to price changes.

    - **Strengths**: The EMA is faster and more sensitive than the SMA, making it a preferred choice for traders in volatile markets who need quicker signals. It's also more suitable for capturing shorter-term price movements.

    - **Weaknesses**: The EMA's sensitivity to recent price changes can lead to more frequent signals, which can sometimes result in more "false positives" during sideways market conditions.

Understanding Moving Averages in Different Timeframes

Moving averages are incredibly versatile because they can be applied to any timeframe, from 1-minute charts for scalpers to daily charts for long-term investors. The key to using them effectively is understanding how their behavior changes with different timeframes:

- **Short-Term Moving Averages**: Moving averages with a short period (e.g., 5, 10, or 20 periods) are more sensitive to price changes. They are ideal for day traders and short-term traders who are looking to capitalize on quick market movements. However, they can be more prone to "whipsaws," where the price quickly reverses direction, triggering false signals.

- **Medium-Term Moving Averages**: A medium-term moving average (e.g., 50-period) strikes a balance between responsiveness and smoothness. It's often used by swing traders who are looking to capture trends over a few days to weeks. It can provide a clearer picture of the trend while avoiding some of the noise seen with short-term averages.

- **Long-Term Moving Averages**: Moving averages with long periods (e.g., 100, 200 periods) are slower to react to price changes but are useful for identifying long-term trends. Investors who focus on the bigger picture may use these averages to confirm the general market direction and to filter out noise from daily price fluctuations.

Advantages and Limitations of Moving Averages

Advantages:

- **Simple to Understand**: Moving averages are straightforward to use and interpret, making them an excellent tool for beginners.

- **Works Well in Trending Markets**: Moving averages are ideal for markets that display clear trends, as they help confirm the market's direction and can highlight potential entry and exit points.

- **Versatile**: They can be used in any market or timeframe, and traders can combine them with other technical indicators for enhanced decision-making.

Limitations:

- **Lagging Indicator**: Since moving averages are based on historical price data, they don't predict future price movements. This lag can result in delayed signals.

- **Not Effective in Sideways Markets**: Moving averages work best in trending markets. In choppy or sideways markets, they can produce false signals (whipsaws) and may not be reliable.

- **False Signals in Volatile Conditions**: Short-term moving averages, while useful in fast-moving markets, can generate a lot of false signals during periods of volatility, requiring traders to be more discerning in their use.

Summary

Moving averages are essential tools in technical analysis that help smooth price fluctuations and reveal the underlying trend. They offer structure in chaotic markets and serve as dynamic support or resistance levels. Whether you're trading fast intraday setups or long-term swings, understanding how moving averages function is foundational for consistent success.

In this chapter, we covered the core concept of moving averages, their types (simple, exponential, and more), and their role in technical trading. This sets the stage for applying moving averages in practical strategies starting in the next chapters.

Key Takeaways

➢ Moving averages help traders visualize market trends by smoothing out price action.

➢ Common types include the **Simple Moving Average (SMA)** and **Exponential Moving Average (EMA)**, each reacting differently to price changes.

➢ Short-period MAs respond quickly to price, while longer-period MAs offer stability and trend confirmation.

➢ Moving averages often act as dynamic **support and resistance** zones.

➢ Understanding moving averages is critical for timing entries, exits, and trend-based decisions.

Chapter 2

Understanding the Advanced Types of Moving Averages

Introduction

Moving averages are the heartbeat of technical analysis, acting as both smoothing mechanisms and dynamic support and resistance zones. But not all moving averages are built the same. To truly master them, you must understand the different types of moving averages, how they're calculated, and how they behave in various market conditions.

In this chapter, we'll explore the most important types of moving averages, their mathematical differences, and how to choose the right type for your strategy. You'll also learn how each one behaves on different timeframes and in different volatility conditions so that you can time entries and exits with precision.

Weighted Moving Average (WMA)

The **Weighted Moving Average (WMA)** assigns the highest weight to the most recent data and lesser weights to older data.

- It smooths price data similarly to an EMA but uses a linear weighting system.
- This type of moving average is especially useful when you want to measure momentum shifts more sharply.
- Because of its calculation method, it can be more complex to apply manually, but trading platforms handle this automatically.

When to use:

- In systems where recent price data needs to be prioritized but still moderately smoothed.
- For momentum-based strategies or during strong directional moves.

Limitations:

- Can exaggerate recent moves and may trigger false entries during pullbacks.
- Not as commonly used as EMA/SMA, so fewer traders monitor it.

Hull Moving Average (HMA)

The **Hull Moving Average (HMA)** was designed to eliminate lag and provide a smoother curve than other averages.

- The HMA uses a weighted calculation and a square root of the period to reduce lag and enhance smoothness.
- It is very responsive to price changes but appears cleaner on charts due to less whipsaw.
- Because of this balance, many traders favor the HMA for both entries and trend confirmation.

When to use:

- When you want smoothness without sacrificing responsiveness.
- In short-term trend trading or scalping strategies.
- When markets are volatile but still show directional intent.

Limitations:

- May not be available on all platforms by default.
- Requires more processing power and may repaint slightly depending on platform settings.

Adaptive Moving Average (AMA / KAMA)

The **Adaptive Moving Average (Kaufman's Adaptive Moving Average or KAMA)** adjusts its sensitivity based on market volatility.

- During trending conditions, the AMA becomes more responsive.
- During consolidations or sideways markets, it flattens out, reducing false signals.
- Its calculation is more complex, using efficiency ratios and smoothing constants.

When to use:

- In strategies that switch between ranging and trending conditions.
- When you want the moving average to self-adjust rather than switching between fast and slow MAs manually.

Limitations:

- Difficult to understand without knowing the math behind it.
- May lag behind EMAs in strong breakout environments.

Comparing Moving Averages by Use Case

Understanding how each moving average type behaves helps you select the best one for your trading style and time horizon.

For Scalping or High-Frequency Trading (1–5 Minute Charts):

- EMAs (e.g., 9 or 21 EMA) for responsiveness
- HMA for fast, smooth feedback

For Intraday Swing Trading (5–30 Minute Charts):

- Combination of EMAs and SMAs
- Use 20 EMA for short-term signals and 50 SMA for trend filtering

For Daily and Higher Timeframe Strategies:

- 50 SMA and 200 SMA for trend structure and longer-term support/resistance
- KAMA if volatility filtering is needed

For Choppy or Range-Bound Markets:

- Avoid EMAs or WMAs unless combined with range filters
- Use adaptive or smoothed averages like KAMA or HMA

Common Moving Average Periods and Their Meaning

Traders across the world often default to specific MA settings. Understanding why they're popular helps you align your charts with widely-followed levels.

- **9 EMA:** Very short-term momentum, commonly used by scalpers
- **20 EMA/SMA:** Captures short-term trends, often aligns with one trading session's average
- **50 EMA/SMA:** Mid-term trend follower; commonly used to filter direction
- **100 SMA:** Reflects broader sentiment; often support/resistance on swing trades
- **200 SMA:** Long-term trend indicator; institutional traders often watch this

These moving averages often act as dynamic support/resistance zones because many market participants reference them.

Combining Moving Averages for Better Signal Confirmation

Using two or more MAs together can help you identify both trend direction and entry/exit points with more confidence.

Popular Combinations:

- **9 EMA and 21 EMA Crossover:** Great for short-term reversals or momentum shifts
- **20 EMA and 50 EMA:** Used for intraday swing confirmation
- **50 SMA and 200 SMA:** Golden Cross (bullish) and Death Cross (bearish) setups

Crossovers Can Signal:

- Trend continuation or reversal
- Entry or exit signals when combined with price action
- Shifts in market structure when aligned with volume

Summary

Understanding the different types of moving averages is foundational for mastering entries and exits. Each type—SMA, EMA, WMA, HMA, and AMA—offers unique characteristics that can serve specific market conditions and trading styles. Selecting the right one for your strategy depends on how reactive you need your signals to be and how much noise you're willing to tolerate. Once you understand how each behaves, you can choose or combine them to suit your preferred timeframe and strategy.

Key Takeaways

➤ **Simple Moving Averages (SMA)** are smooth and slow, best for filtering noise and identifying long-term trends.

➤ **Exponential Moving Averages (EMA)** respond quickly to price action and are ideal for short-term strategies.

➤ **Weighted and Hull MAs** offer faster response times but can introduce more false signals in choppy markets.

➤ **Kaufman's Adaptive MA (KAMA)** adjusts to market volatility, offering dynamic filtering during ranging vs trending conditions.

➤ Combining moving averages (like 9 EMA with 21 EMA or 50 SMA with 200 SMA) can provide more reliable trend confirmation and crossover signals.

➤ Each moving average has strengths and weaknesses—your job is to align their behavior with your trading goals and risk tolerance.

Chapter 3

Combining Moving Averages with Price Action – Creating a Dynamic Trading Edge

Introduction

Moving averages are powerful tools on their own, but when combined with price action techniques, they unlock deeper insight into market behavior. This chapter focuses on integrating moving averages with price structure, candlestick patterns, and market context to refine your entries and exits with greater precision. You'll learn how to read the story behind the price and let the moving averages act as dynamic guides—not rigid rules.

Why Combine Moving Averages with Price Action?

- Moving averages smooth out price data, but they lack context on their own.
- Price action provides the raw structure of the market: higher highs, lower lows, consolidations, breakouts, and fakeouts.
- When used together, moving averages offer trend guidance while price action confirms or invalidates trade ideas.

Key Concepts of Price Action

- **Support and Resistance Levels**: Areas where price historically reacts—either bouncing off or breaking through.

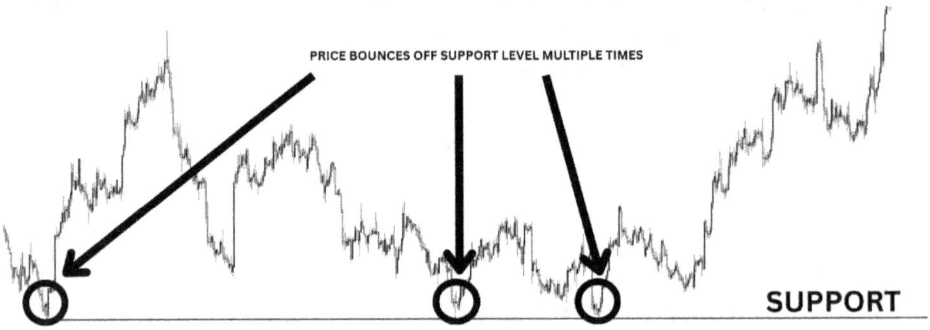

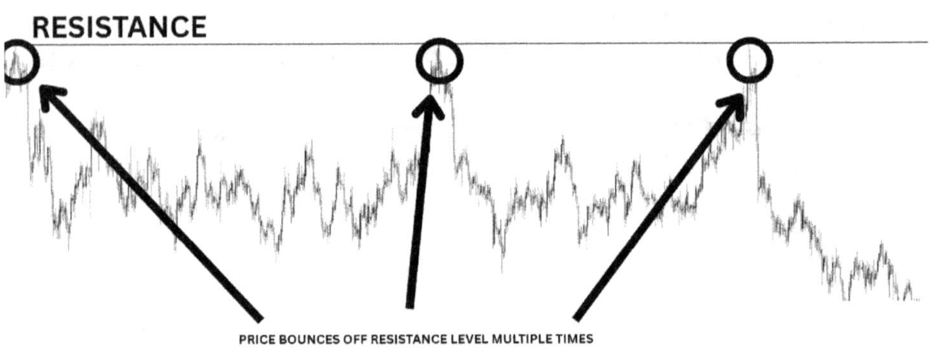

- **Trend Structure**: A market in an uptrend should make higher highs and higher lows; a downtrend should make lower highs and lower lows. Moving averages should align with this structure to validate the trend.

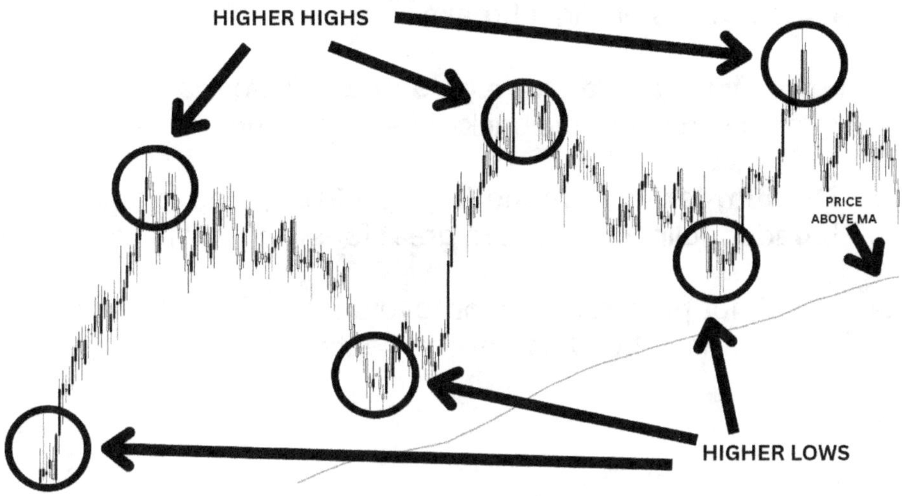

- **Candlestick Reversals**: Patterns like pin bars, engulfing candles, and inside bars can serve as precise entry or exit signals when near a key moving average.

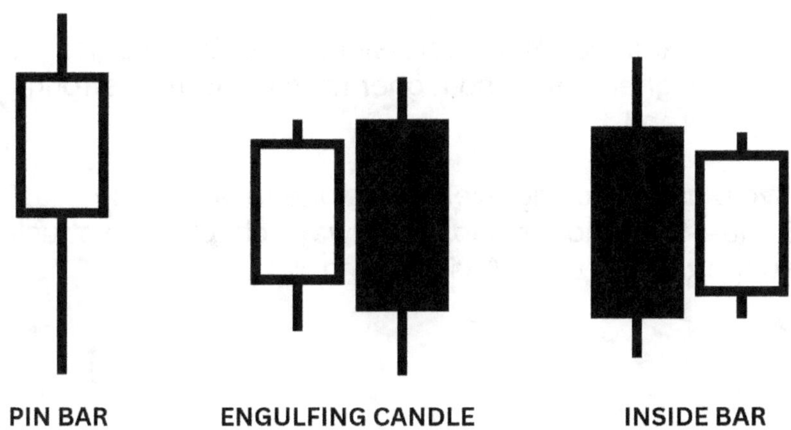

Using Moving Averages as Dynamic Support and Resistance

- Moving averages act like “zones” rather than precise levels. Expect wicks or slight breaks—not exact bounces.
- **Short-term averages (e.g., 9 or 21 EMA)** react quickly and often catch minor pullbacks in strong trends.
- **Medium-term averages (e.g., 50 SMA)** tend to hold in broader pullbacks and are great for swing trading strategies.
- Watch for price rejection or reversal candles when touching these MAs in trending environments.

Trend Confirmation with Moving Averages + Structure

- Confirm a trend using both the slope of the moving average and the pattern of price action.
    - Example: An upward-sloping 20 EMA combined with higher highs and higher lows confirms a strong bullish trend.
- Avoid using moving averages alone to determine trend—false moves happen. Always check if the structure supports what the MA is showing.

Combining Moving Averages with Entry Candles

- Use candle signals near MAs to time trades:
  - **Bullish Engulfing at 21 EMA in uptrend**: Potential reversal signal, consider entry with tight stop below candle low.

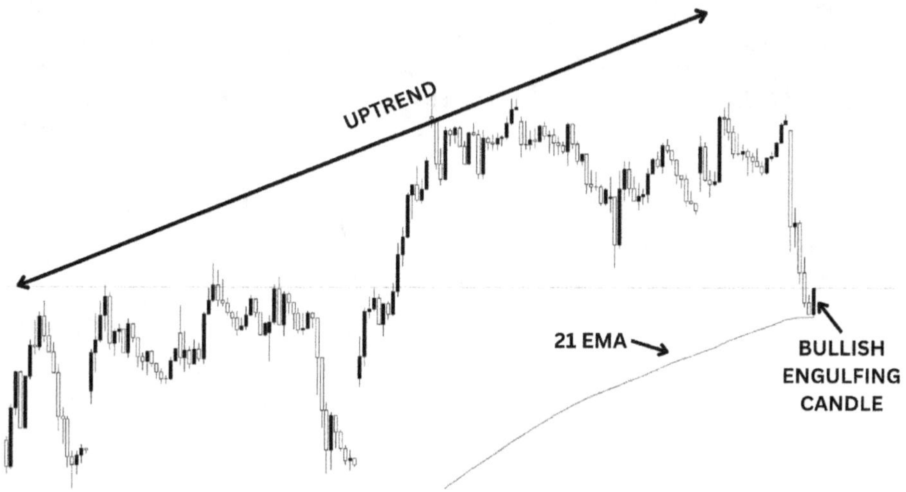

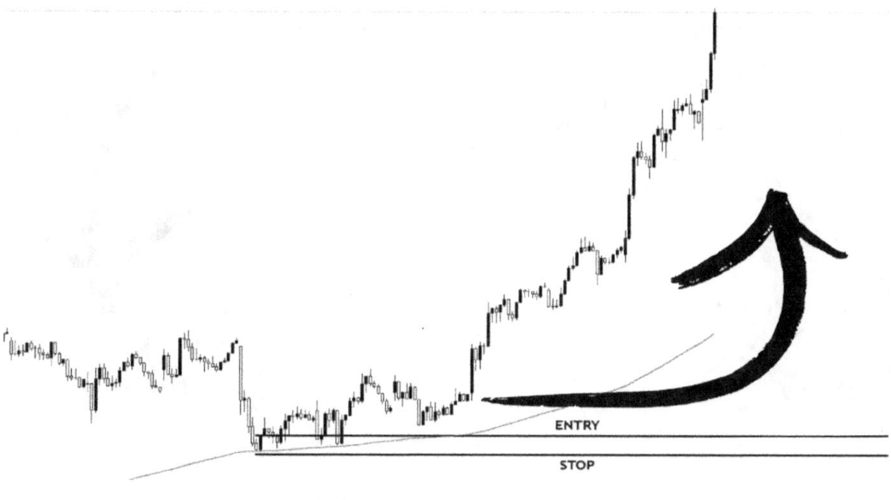

- **Bearish Pin Bar at 50 EMA in downtrend**: Potential reversal signal, especially if at a lower high. Consider an entry with a tight stop above candle low.

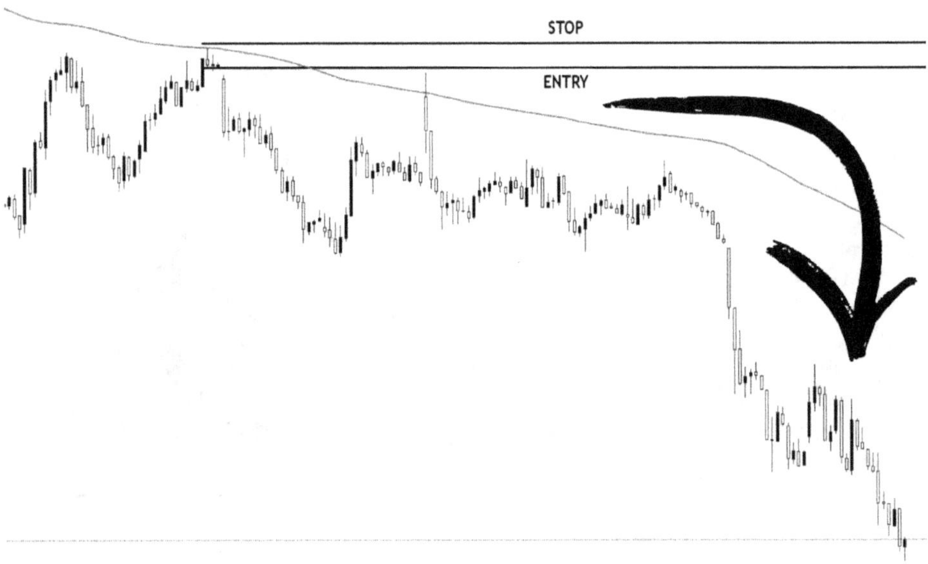

- Ideal setups combine:
    - Confluence of MA + Support/Resistance + Candlestick Pattern
    - Example: Price pulls back to 50 SMA + horizontal support + bullish engulfing candle → High-probability long setup.

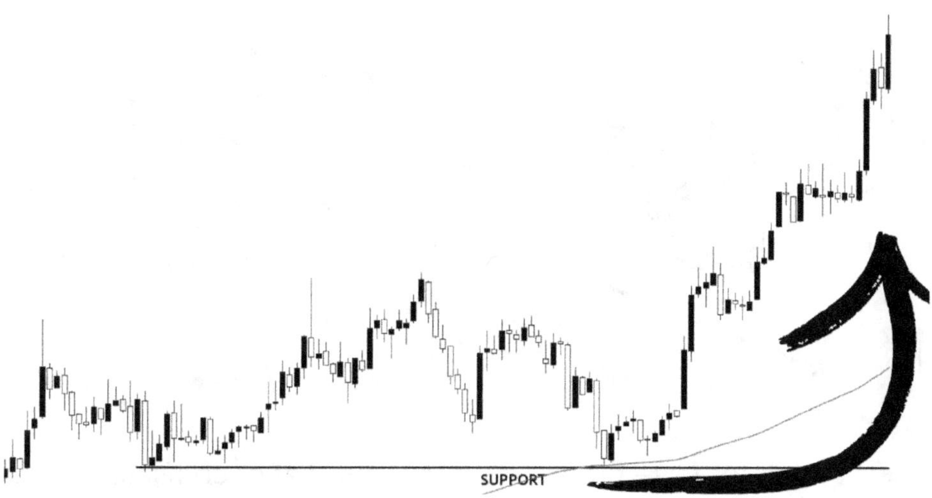

Breakouts and Moving Averages

- Moving averages help spot pre-breakout consolidation zones.
- Use them as a filter for breakout direction:
    - If price consolidates above a rising 20 EMA, and a bullish breakout occurs → High likelihood of continuation.

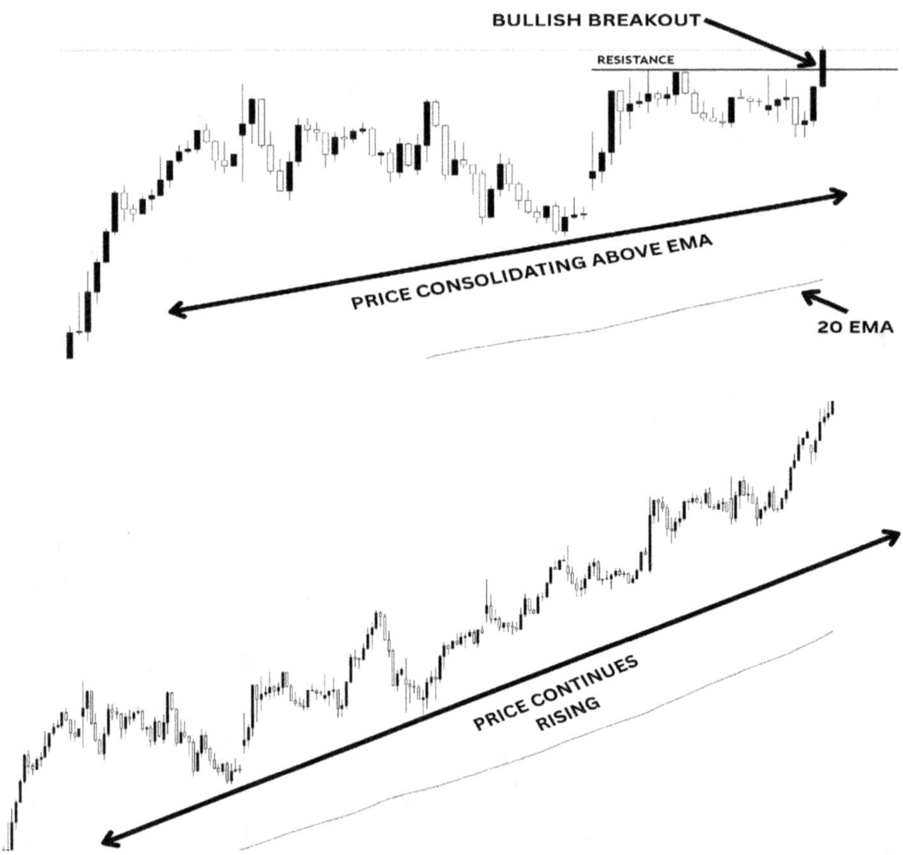

- Watch for false breakouts if MAs are flat or conflicting across multiple timeframes.

Filtering False Signals with Context

- Avoid blindly buying every candle touch on the moving average.
- Confirm with:
    - Volume spikes supporting direction
    - Candlestick strength (e.g., strong closes)
    - Overall market trend (use higher timeframes for confirmation)
- Moving averages can lag—don't trade in isolation.

Summary

Combining moving averages with price action gives traders an edge by blending trend-following indicators with the raw narrative of the market. Instead of relying on one tool, this integrated approach allows for precise entries, better exits, and greater confidence in market structure. From candlestick confirmation to identifying fakeouts and pullbacks, this strategy helps refine timing while staying aligned with momentum.

Key Takeaways

➢ Moving averages are more powerful when used alongside price action, structure, and candlestick patterns.

➢ Use MAs as dynamic zones of support/resistance, not exact levels.

➢ Confirm trends using both moving averages and the pattern of price (higher highs/lows or lower highs/lows).

➢ Ideal trade setups form when a candlestick reversal pattern aligns with MA support/resistance and broader market context.

➢ Avoid trading solely based on moving average touches—use context like volume, structure, and higher timeframes to validate setups.

Chapter 4

Dynamic Support and Resistance – Mastering Market Structure with Moving Averages

Introduction

In the ever-changing landscape of the financial markets, understanding how price reacts to support and resistance is fundamental. While traditional support and resistance are typically drawn as horizontal lines, moving averages offer a *dynamic* way to measure these levels. Because they adapt with price over time, moving averages give traders a real-time read on where buyers and sellers are likely to step in. This chapter explores how to identify, interpret, and capitalize on dynamic support and resistance using various moving averages across different market conditions.

What is Dynamic Support and Resistance?

- Traditional support and resistance are often seen as static levels where price has historically reversed or paused.
- Dynamic support and resistance change with time—they shift as the market evolves.
- Moving averages act as these shifting barriers, offering insight into the current sentiment of market participants.

Why Moving Averages Work as Support and Resistance

- Moving averages are widely used by institutions, retail traders, and algorithms, which creates self-fulfilling price reactions around them.
- In uptrends, commonly used moving averages like the 20 EMA or 50 SMA often act as support zones where buyers look to re-enter.

- In downtrends, the same moving averages can act as resistance, repelling price back down when sellers defend those zones.

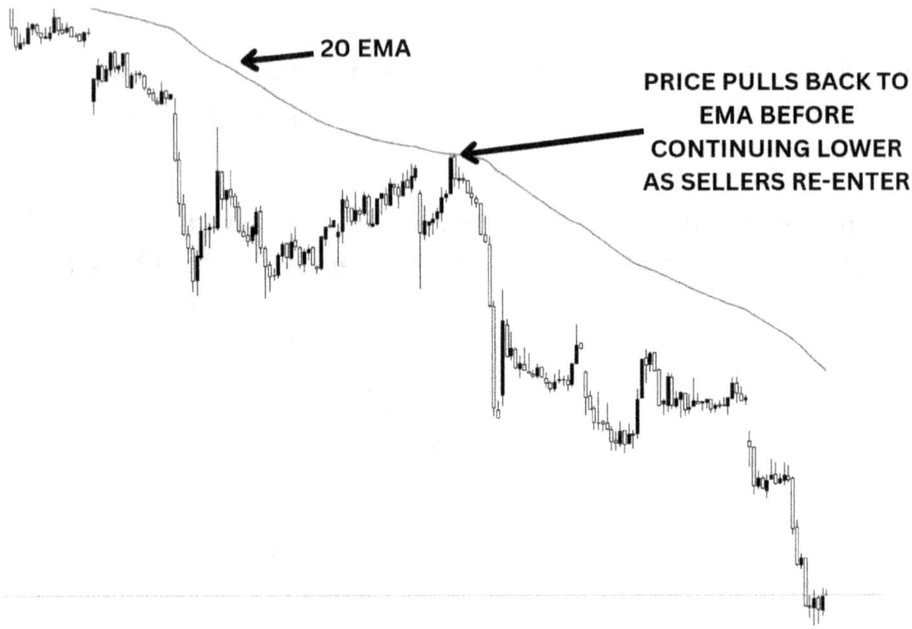

- The number of times price reacts to a moving average increases its significance.

Choosing the Right Moving Average for Dynamic Levels

Different types and lengths of moving averages behave differently as support and resistance. Choosing the right one for your timeframe and strategy is crucial:

- **Short-Term (Fast) MAs** like the 9 or 20 EMA:
    - Best for scalping and momentum trading.
    - React quickly to price changes and offer early entries during trends.
    - Often retested in strong trends with shallow pullbacks.

- **Medium-Term MAs** like the 50 SMA or 50 EMA:
    - Good for swing traders and multi-day setups.
    - Provide support or resistance in established trends with deeper pullbacks.

- **Long-Term MAs** like the 100 and 200 SMA:
    - Useful for position traders or confirming broader trend direction.
    - Frequently tested during larger corrections or macro shifts.

How to Identify Valid Dynamic Levels

Spotting strong moving average zones is part art and part science. Consider these criteria:

- **Multiple Touches Without a Break**: If a moving average has acted as support or resistance multiple times, it gains credibility.
- **Confluence with Price Action**: When a moving average aligns with a prior high/low, trendline, or Fibonacci level, its strength is amplified.
- **Volume Confirmation**: Strong reactions from MAs accompanied by high volume suggest institutional participation.

Interpreting Price Behavior Around Moving Averages

Understanding how price interacts with a moving average can provide clues about future market direction:

- **Clean Bounces**: These often signal strong trends and provide ideal entries.
- **Wicks and Shadows**: When price pierces an MA but closes back above or below it, it shows the level is still being respected.
- **Breaks with Momentum**: If price slices through an MA on strong volume, it may signal a trend reversal or acceleration.

Entry Strategies Using Dynamic Support and Resistance

There are several powerful entry techniques using moving averages as a bounce or breakout tool:

- **Pullback Entries**:
  - Wait for price to retrace to a trending MA (like the 20 or 50 EMA).
  - Confirm the bounce with a bullish engulfing candle, hammer, or volume surge.
  - Place stop-loss just below the moving average or recent swing low.

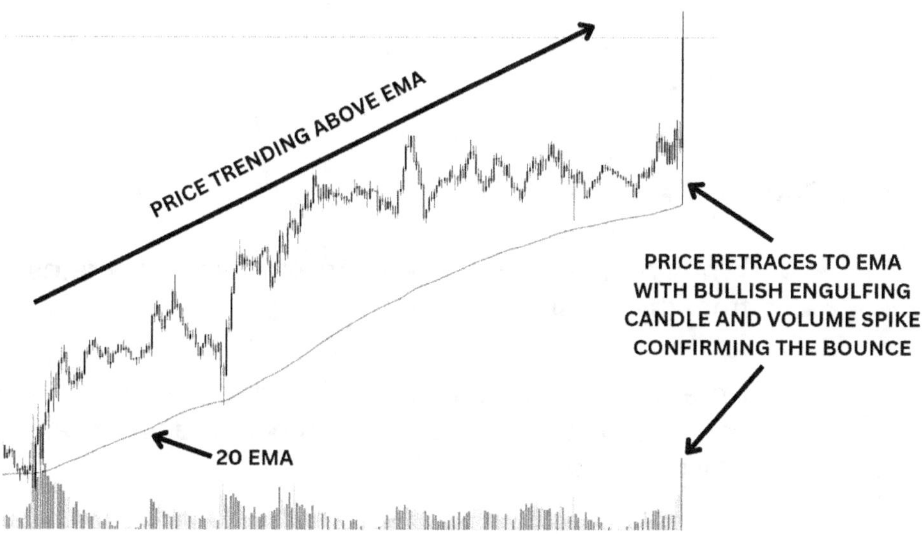

- **Breakout Retests**:
    - When a moving average is broken, wait for a retest from the other side.
    - Enter when price tests the MA and rejects it, confirming its new role (support becomes resistance or vice versa).
    - Place stop-loss just above the moving average or recent swing high.

PRICE BREAKS
BELOW EMA
21 EMA

PRICE RISES
BACK UP TO AND
BOUNCES OFF
THE EMA

STOP
ENTRY

- **Stacked MAs Strategy**:
  - In strong trends, use stacked moving averages (e.g., 9 EMA above 20 EMA above 50 EMA).
  - Enter on pullbacks to the shortest MA in the stack, using the others as layered support. Place stop below the longest EMA to avoid getting stopped out before the reversal.

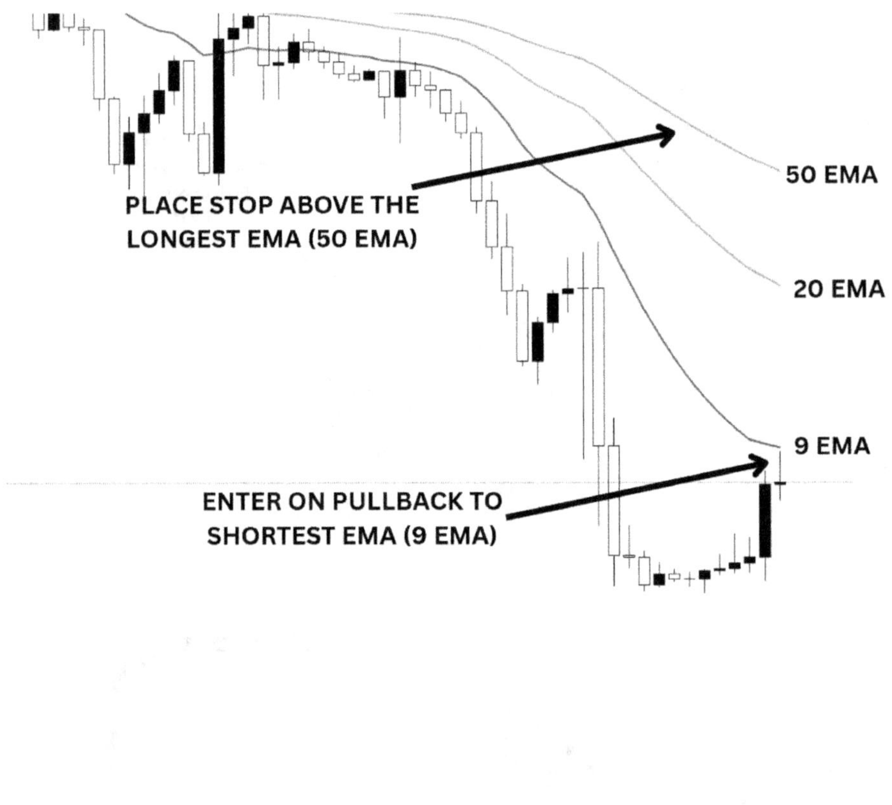

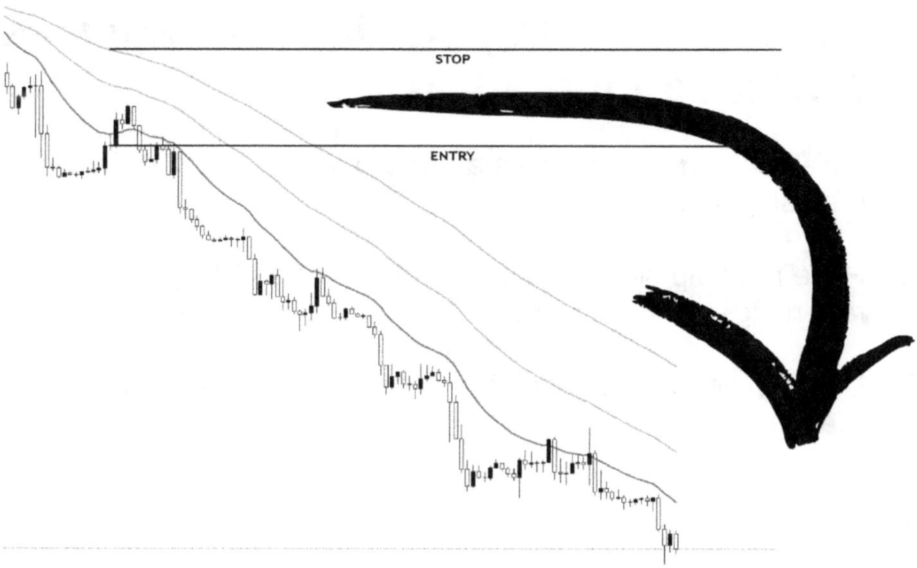

Common Mistakes When Trading Dynamic Levels

Avoiding these pitfalls can improve your use of MAs as support and resistance:

- **Blindly Buying at Every MA**: Wait for confirmation; don't assume every touch will hold.
- **Ignoring Trend Strength**: MAs are less reliable in choppy, sideways markets—avoid trading them in low-volatility conditions.
- **Overloading Charts with MAs**: Too many MAs can create confusion and conflicting signals. Stick to 2–3 that suit your strategy.

Advanced Tip: Using Moving Averages as a Zone, Not a Line

- Treat moving averages as a **zone** of interest rather than a precise level.
- Price may dip slightly below or above an MA before reversing—this is normal.
- Use candlestick confirmation or volume spikes to confirm reactions.

Summary

- Moving averages act as dynamic support and resistance that evolve with price.
- Different moving averages serve different purposes based on timeframe and strategy.
- Valid MA levels show repeated reactions and often align with other technical tools.
- You can use moving averages to build high-probability entries, exits, and risk strategies.
- Avoid overreliance on moving averages in sideways markets or without confirmation.

Key Takeaways

➤ Moving averages are powerful tools for identifying dynamic support and resistance levels that shift with the market.

➤ Use short-term MAs (9, 20 EMA) for fast-moving strategies, medium MAs (50 EMA/SMA) for swing trading, and long-term MAs (100, 200 SMA) for macro structure.

➤ Strong price reactions to MAs—especially when confirmed by volume or other tools—often lead to tradeable setups.

➤ Entries can be made on clean MA bounces, retests after breakouts, or when MAs are stacked in a trend.

➤ Use MAs for trailing stops, exit signals, and as reference points for risk management.

➤ Don't treat moving averages as hard lines—price often interacts with them as zones.

Chapter 5

Moving Average Envelopes – Expanding the Boundaries of Trend Analysis

Introduction

Moving averages are powerful tools on their own, but their true versatility shines when paired with envelope techniques. Moving Average Envelopes (MAEs) form dynamic bands above and below a central moving average to represent volatility, overbought/oversold zones, and trend strength. These envelopes give traders a more adaptive view of the market and allow for precision entries, exits, and reversals based on price behavior relative to these bands.

In this chapter, we'll explore how Moving Average Envelopes work, how they differ from Bollinger Bands, and how to apply them to futures and equity markets to get ahead of the curve.

What Are Moving Average Envelopes?

- Moving Average Envelopes consist of a central moving average with two outer bands placed a fixed percentage above and below the average.
- These bands serve as visual boundaries that help traders identify potential extremes in price movement.
- Unlike Bollinger Bands, which adjust based on standard deviation, envelopes maintain a constant distance from the average.

Core Components of MA Envelopes

- **Central Line:** This is the main moving average, which can be a simple, exponential, or weighted MA.
- **Upper Envelope:** A fixed percentage (e.g., +2%) above the moving average, potentially signaling an overbought market.
- **Lower Envelope:** A fixed percentage (e.g., -2%) below the moving average, potentially signaling an oversold condition.
- **Envelope Width:** Traders must choose an appropriate percentage to capture natural price swings without creating noise.

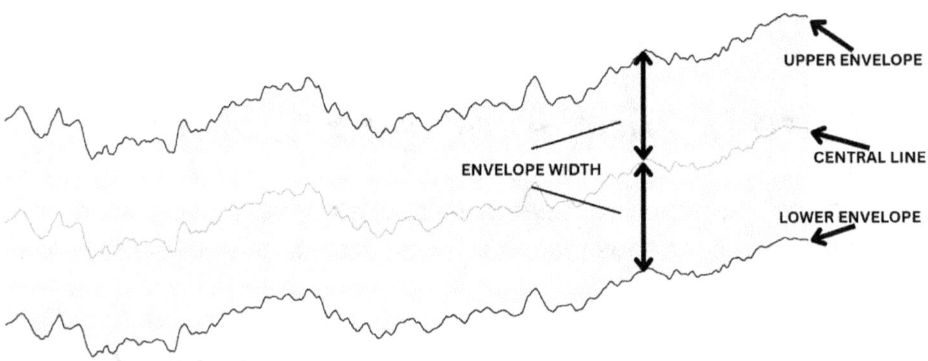

Why Use Moving Average Envelopes?

- Help identify **price extremes** relative to a trend, improving timing for mean reversion or trend continuation trades.
- Allow traders to spot **overextension** in trending markets that may lead to pullbacks or corrections.
- Offer **visual boundaries** to manage risk and define exit levels, especially for countertrend traders.
- Can help avoid false signals that often occur when relying on a single moving average.

Comparing Envelopes vs. Bollinger Bands

- Bollinger Bands adapt based on **standard deviation** — they expand and contract with market volatility.
- Envelopes remain a **fixed percentage**, offering stability and clarity in trending markets.
- Bollinger Bands are better for **volatility-based strategies**, while envelopes are stronger for **trend-following and range-trading strategies**.

How to Set Envelope Percentages

- There's no one-size-fits-all setting. Traders must experiment to fit the asset and timeframe.
- **For intraday futures trading**, envelopes between 0.5% and 1.5% work well on major contracts like CL (oil), ES (S&P 500), or GC (gold).
- **For swing trading**, 2% to 3% is more common due to broader price movement.
- Adjust width based on volatility—more volatile markets may require wider envelopes to avoid frequent whipsaws.

MA Envelope Strategies for Entry and Exit

- **Pullback Entry:** Enter on price touching the lower envelope during an uptrend, or the upper envelope during a downtrend.

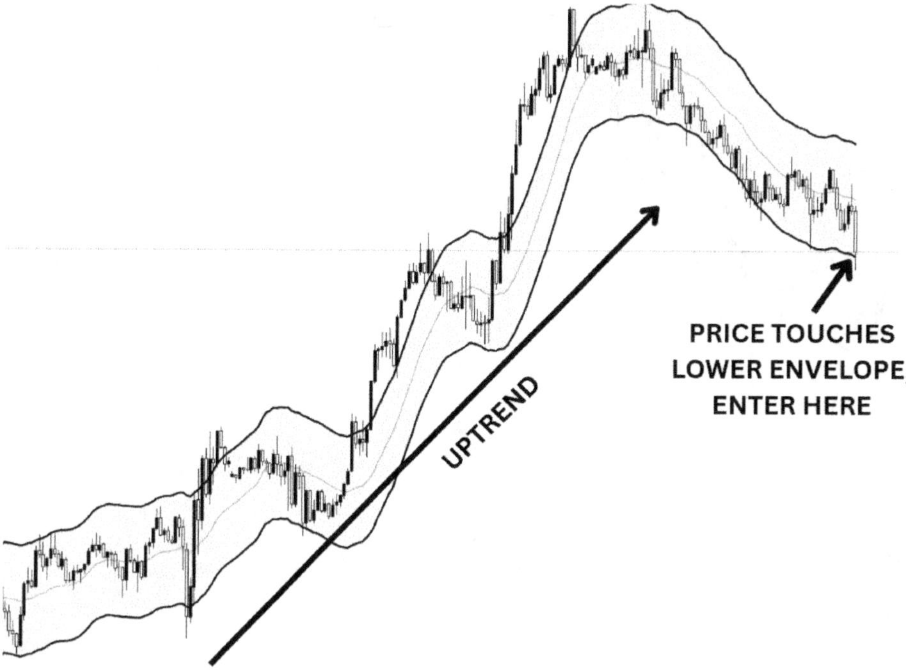

- **Reversion to Mean Exit:** Exit trades as price reverts back to the central MA.

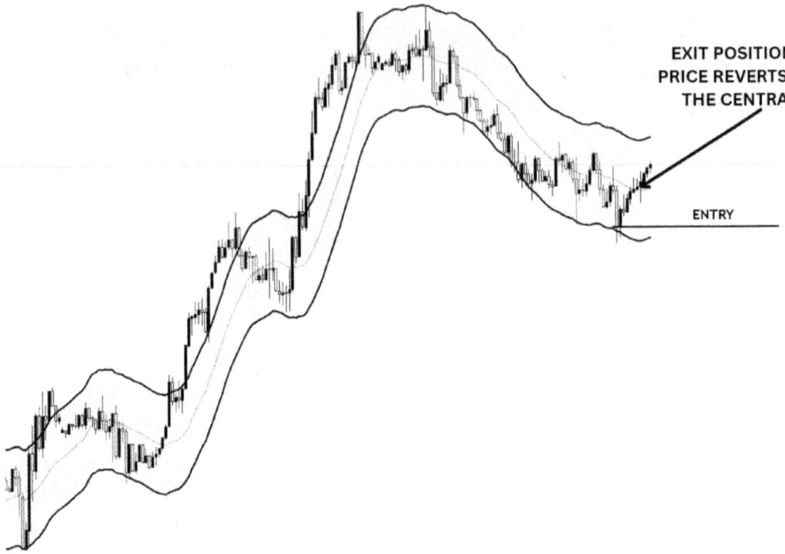

- **Breakout Entry:** Use envelope breakouts as confirmation of trend continuation after a consolidation. Enter the trade after a break above the upper band, or vice versa.

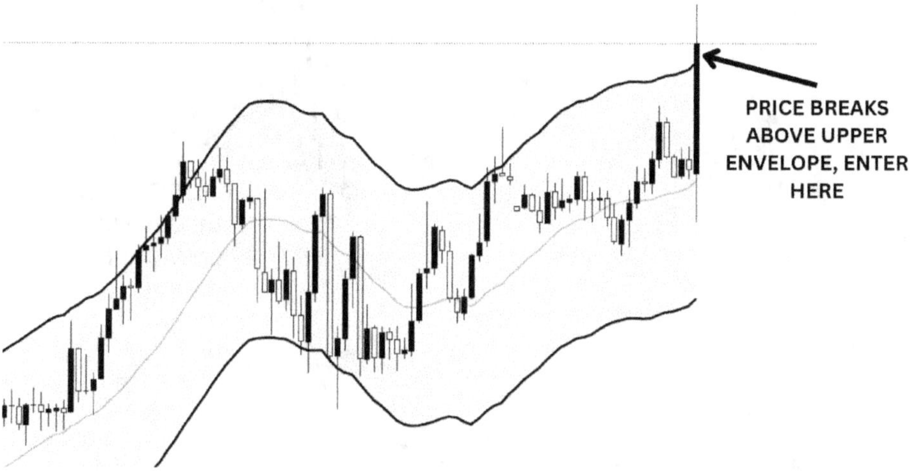

- **Trailing Stop Tool:** Use the envelope as a dynamic trailing stop—stay in the trade as long as price respects the outer band, exit as soon as price crosses back below or above the outer band.

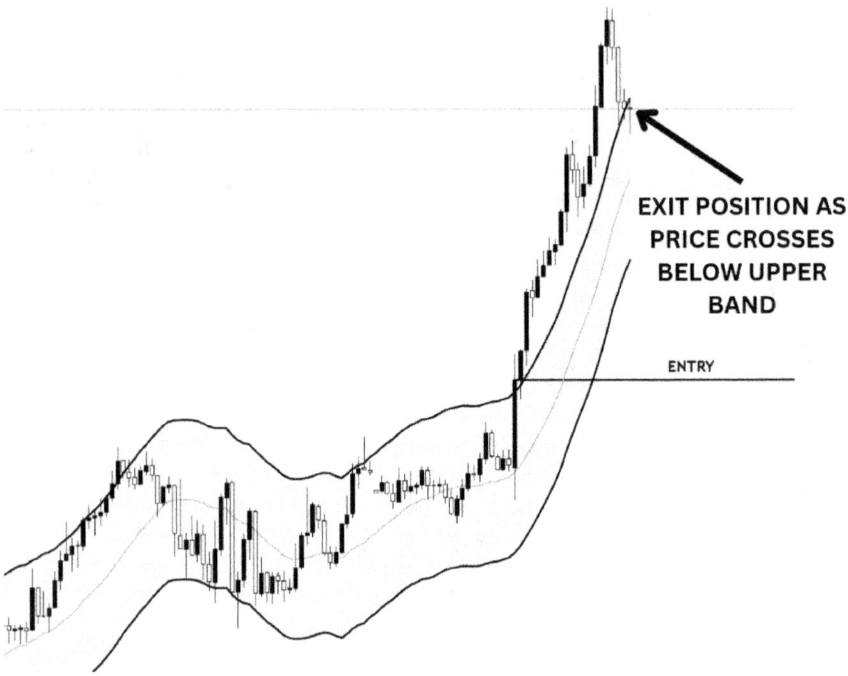

Filtering with Volume and Momentum

- Combine envelopes with **volume indicators** like On-Balance Volume or Volume Oscillator to confirm breakout strength.
- Pair with **momentum tools** like RSI or MACD to avoid fading strong trends.
- Example: If price touches the upper envelope and RSI is overbought, you may consider a short position—but only if volume starts to decline.

Backtesting and Optimization

- Backtest envelope strategies using historical data across different volatility environments.
- Optimize your envelope percentage for each instrument. For instance:
    - Crude oil may work well with ±1.25% envelopes on the 5-minute chart.
    - Gold may be better suited to ±1.5% envelopes on the hourly chart.
- Combine with other moving average filters (like the 50 EMA) to reduce false signals.

Limitations and Risk Considerations

- Static envelopes can lag behind sudden volatility shifts, leading to whipsaws.
- Requires proper **stop-loss rules** when fading price extremes—trending markets can run far beyond outer bands.
- Not suited for all assets—envelopes are most effective on **liquid, moderately volatile** markets.

Summary

Moving Average Envelopes provide a powerful extension to classic moving average strategies by adding structure to market extremes. With carefully chosen percentages and smart combinations with volume and momentum tools, traders can spot high-probability setups, manage risk, and gain a broader perspective of trend health. Whether you're trading reversals, continuations, or breakouts, envelopes offer clarity and consistency in strategy execution.

Key Takeaways

➢ Moving Average Envelopes consist of upper and lower bands set at a fixed percentage above and below a central moving average.

➢ They help identify overbought and oversold zones in a trending or ranging market.

➢ Unlike Bollinger Bands, envelopes do not expand with volatility, offering stability for trend-following strategies.

➢ Ideal envelope percentages vary by asset and time frame—start with 1%–2% and adjust based on backtesting results.

➢ Envelopes work best when combined with volume or momentum indicators to filter high-probability trades.

➢ Use envelopes as dynamic support/resistance levels and trailing stops to enhance risk management.

Chapter 6

Moving Average Crossovers – Timing Momentum Shifts with Confidence

Introduction

One of the most widely used techniques among technical traders is the moving average crossover. At its core, this strategy is based on watching two (or more) moving averages with different lengths and identifying when they cross each other. These crossovers act as signals—either to enter a new trend or to confirm a momentum shift. While the concept is simple, the technique requires nuance, timing, and proper filtering to avoid false signals. This chapter dives deep into how crossovers work, the most effective combinations, and how to integrate them into your trading strategy.

What Is a Moving Average Crossover?

- A moving average crossover occurs when a short-term moving average crosses above or below a longer-term moving average.
- It is commonly used to spot trend reversals, trend continuation setups, or confirmation of momentum shifts.
- These signals are popular in both discretionary and algorithmic trading systems due to their rule-based nature.

Why Crossovers Work

- Crossovers capture the **relationship between momentum and price direction**.
- When a faster MA crosses a slower MA from below, it typically signals that short-term price action has gained bullish strength.
- When it crosses from above, it can indicate bearish momentum is accelerating.
- Institutions and retail traders alike monitor key crossover signals, contributing to their effectiveness.

Common Crossover Setups

- **Golden Cross**:
    - Occurs when the 50-day EMA crosses above the 200-day EMA.
    - This is a long-term bullish signal often used by investors and swing traders.

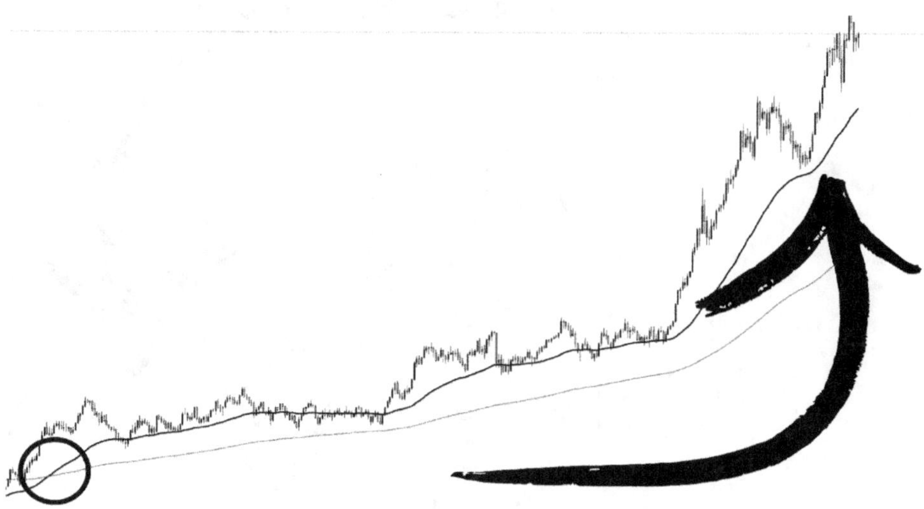

- **Death Cross**:
    - Occurs when the 50-day EMA crosses below the 200-day EMA.
    - Signals a potential long-term downtrend.

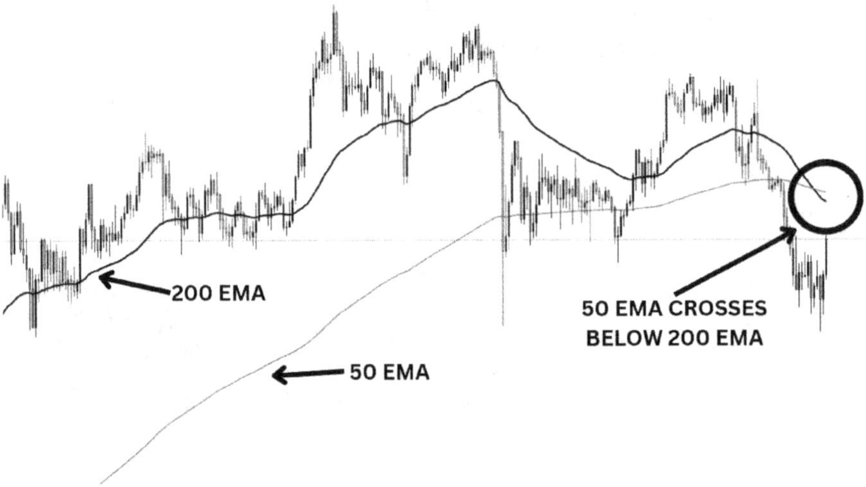

- **9/20 EMA Crossover**:
    - A popular short-term setup used for day trading and swing trading.
    - The 9 EMA crossing above the 20 EMA indicates momentum is shifting bullishly and vice versa.

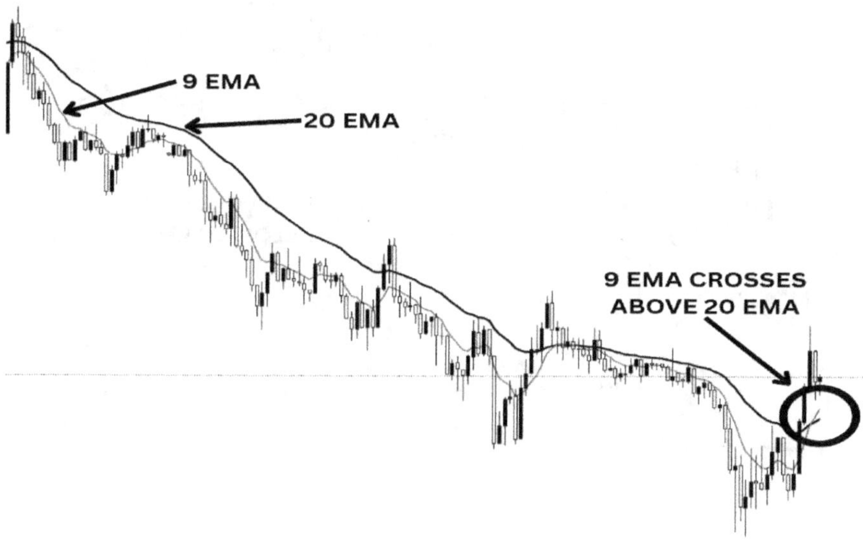

- **Fast Crossovers (e.g., 5 EMA & 10 EMA)**:
    - More reactive, providing earlier entries and exits.
    - Often used in scalping and high-frequency strategies but can generate more false signals.

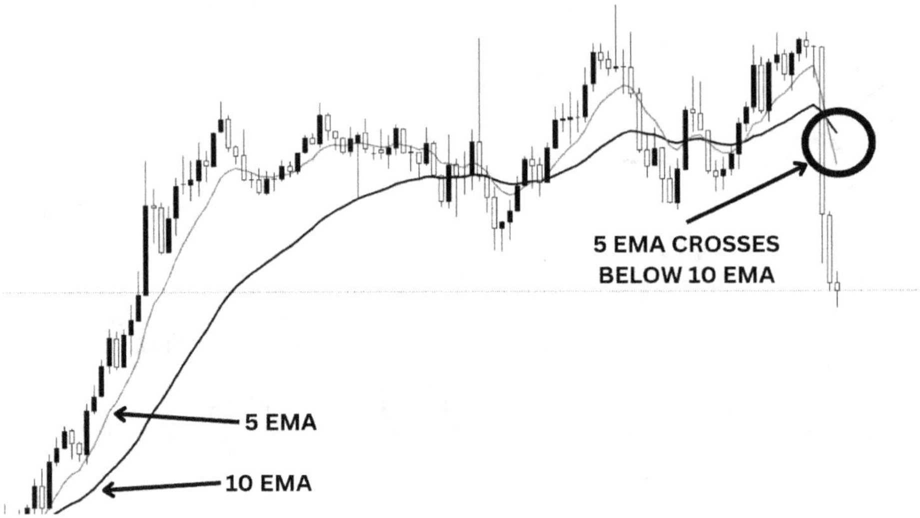

Interpreting Crossovers in Different Market Conditions

- **Trending Markets**:
  - Crossovers are more reliable in strong, directional markets.
  - Look for clear trend structure with higher highs and higher lows (for bullish setups).

- **Choppy or Range-Bound Markets**:
  - Crossovers can produce many false signals due to rapid, non-directional movement.
  - Consider using filters such as RSI or ADX to confirm that a trend is in place.

- **Volatile Conditions**:
  - In high volatility, fast MAs can whip around, causing frequent false crossovers.
  - Smoothing techniques or longer MAs can help mitigate noise.

Filtering and Confirming Crossover Signals

To increase the reliability of crossover entries:

- **Use Volume Confirmation**:
    - A crossover that happens on increased volume is more likely to be valid.

- **Add Momentum Indicators**:
    - Use RSI, MACD, or Stochastic to confirm that momentum is supporting the crossover.

- **Identify Market Context**:
    - Only take bullish crossovers in uptrends and bearish crossovers in downtrends.
    - Avoid trading against the dominant trend.

Entry Techniques with Crossovers

Here are practical ways to enter a trade once a crossover signal occurs:

- **Aggressive Entry**:
  - Enter as soon as the crossover occurs.
  - Offers early positioning but comes with more risk of false signals.

- **Conservative Entry**:
  - Wait for a pullback after the crossover and enter on confirmation (e.g., a bullish engulfing candle).
  - This reduces risk but may cause you to miss the early part of the move.

- **Breakout Entry**:
  - Combine crossovers with horizontal breakout levels.
  - If a crossover occurs near a resistance zone, wait for a break above before entering.

Exit Strategies for Crossover Trades

Effective exits can maximize gains and limit risk:

- **Exit on Opposite Crossover**:
    - For example, exit a long position when the short MA crosses below the long MA.

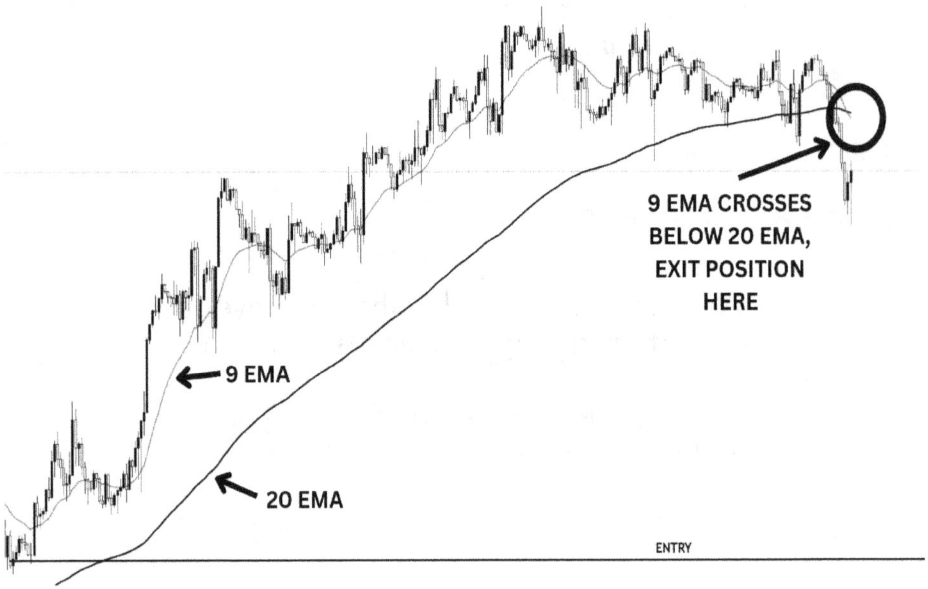

- **Use a Trailing Stop with MA Support**:
    - Let a shorter moving average trail the price and exit when price closes below it.

- **Set Targets at Major MAs or Price Structure**:
    - Use longer-term MAs (like 100 or 200 SMA) or previous highs/lows to define exit zones.

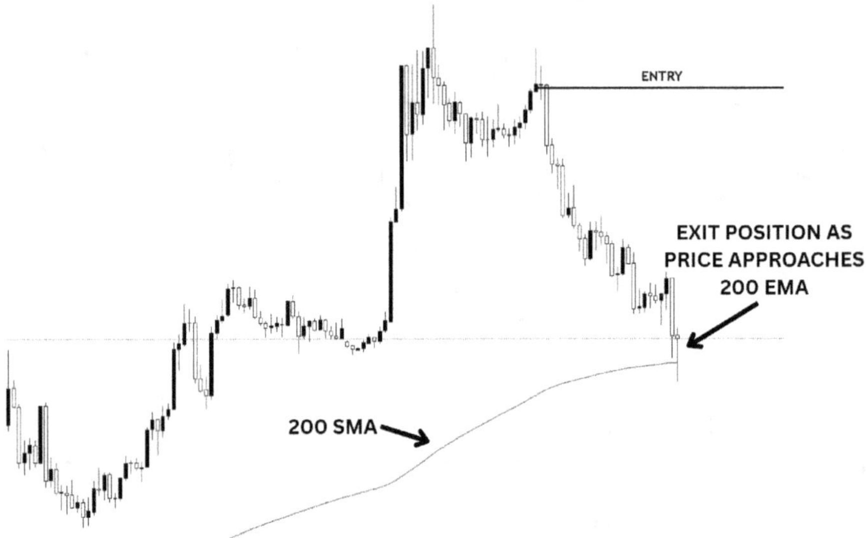

Pros and Cons of Using Crossover Strategies

Pros:

- Simple and rule-based—ideal for new and experienced traders.
- Useful in trend-following and momentum-based systems.
- Can be automated or traded manually.

Cons:

- Prone to whipsaws in choppy markets.
- Lagging nature may result in late entries or exits.
- Requires confirmation tools to be more effective.

Advanced Crossover Concepts

- **Triple MA Crossover**:
  - Involves three moving averages (e.g., 9 EMA, 20 EMA, and 50 SMA).
  - Strongest signals occur when all three are stacked in the same direction and then cross.

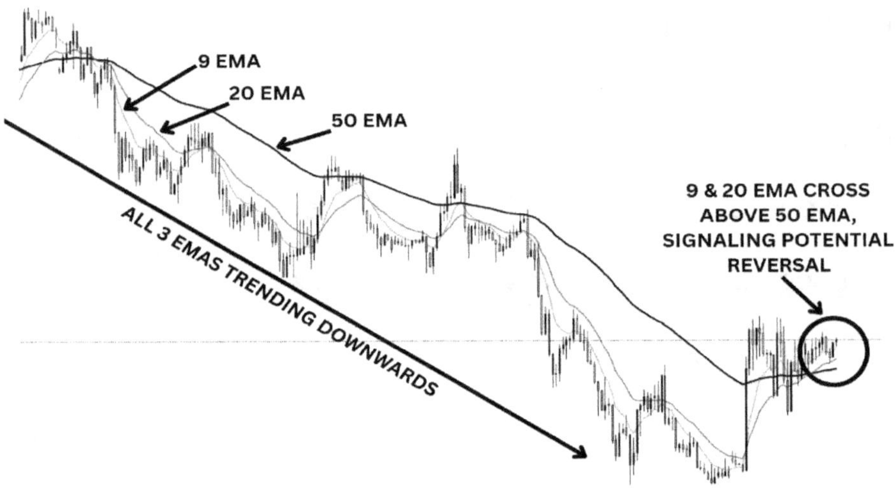

- **EMA/SMA Combo**:
    - Combine an exponential MA with a simple MA for different sensitivities.
    - Example: 9 EMA crossing above the 50 SMA can catch shifts early while smoothing noise.
- **Crossover Zones**:
    - Don't treat the crossover as a single price point—look for confirmation across several candles or with other indicators.

Summary

- Moving average crossovers are effective tools for identifying trend changes and momentum shifts.
- Common combinations like the 9/20 EMA or the 50/200 SMA offer powerful signals in the right context.
- Crossovers work best in trending markets and require filtering in sideways conditions.
- Entry and exit techniques can be tailored based on your risk tolerance and market volatility.
- Confirming with momentum indicators, volume, or price structure enhances the reliability of crossovers.

Key Takeaways

➤ Moving average crossovers involve the intersection of short-term and long-term MAs to signal potential trend shifts.

➤ The Golden Cross and Death Cross are classic long-term signals, while 9/20 EMA crossovers are ideal for shorter timeframes.

➤ Crossovers are most effective in trending markets and require filtering in sideways or volatile conditions.

➤ Entries can be aggressive (at the cross), conservative (on a pullback), or confirmatory (on a breakout).

➤ Exits can be based on reverse crossovers, trailing MA stops, or price targets aligned with structure or other MAs.

➤ Use volume, momentum indicators, and market context to reduce the chance of false crossover signals.

Chapter 7

Combining Moving Averages with Volume – Uncover Powerful Trade Confirmations

Introduction

Moving averages are powerful on their own, but when combined with volume analysis, they become even more effective at filtering false signals and confirming strong trade setups. Volume is often considered the "fuel" behind price movement—without significant volume, price action can be misleading. In this chapter, we'll explore how pairing moving averages with volume indicators can enhance your entry and exit timing and help you stay on the right side of the market.

Why Volume Matters in Trading

- Volume measures how many contracts, shares, or units are traded over a given period. It represents the strength or conviction behind a price move.
- A price breakout or breakdown with **low volume** may indicate a false move or lack of trader participation.
- A breakout or trend continuation with **high volume** suggests strong institutional or trader interest and increases the likelihood of follow-through.

The Relationship Between Volume and Moving Averages

- Moving averages smooth out price action, and volume confirms the **validity** of that price action.
- When price crosses a key moving average, volume helps determine whether the move is likely to sustain or reverse.
- Volume can act as a **second filter** to validate signals produced by moving averages.

Volume Confirmation for Moving Average Crossovers

- A common strategy is the **moving average crossover**, such as when the 9 EMA crosses above the 21 EMA (bullish) or below (bearish).
- Use volume spikes during these crossovers as confirmation:
    - A **bullish crossover** with increased volume suggests strong buying interest.

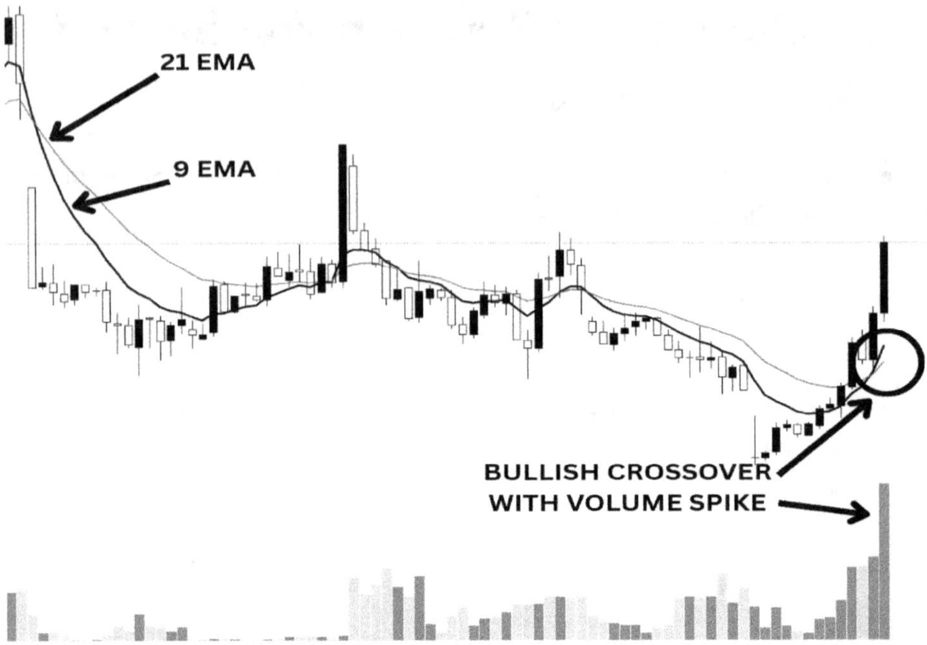
21 EMA
9 EMA
BULLISH CROSSOVER
WITH VOLUME SPIKE

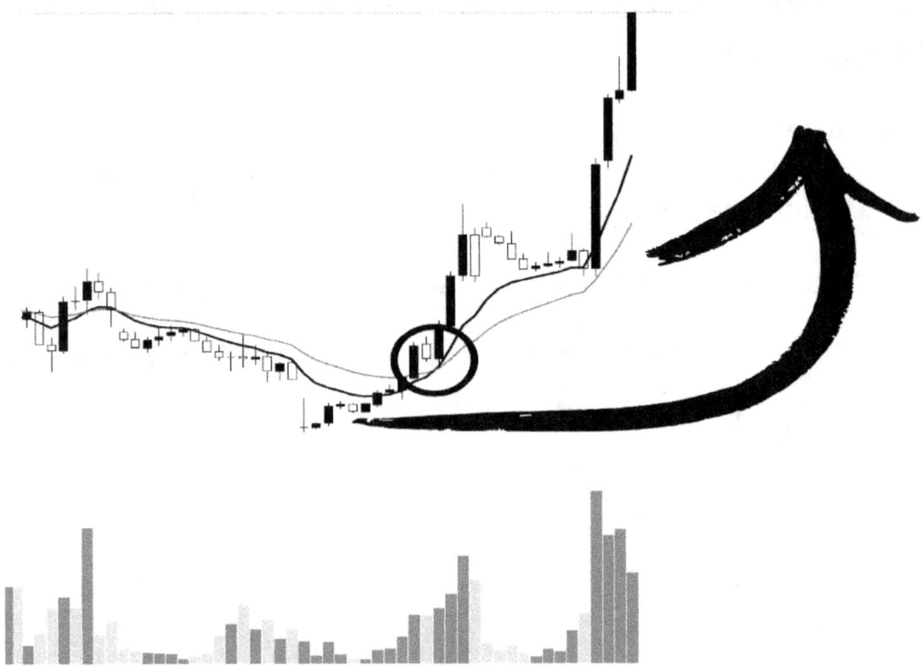

- A **bearish crossover** with high volume suggests strong selling pressure.

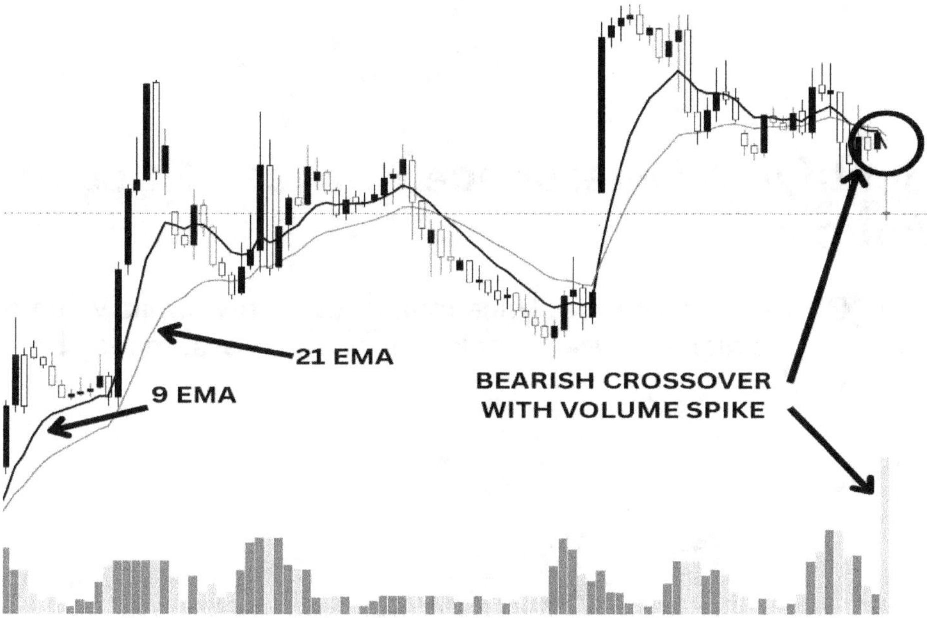

- If volume remains flat or decreases during the crossover, it may signal a lack of conviction and a higher chance of a reversal.

Identifying Divergence Between Price and Volume

- **Bullish divergence:** Price makes lower lows while volume makes higher lows—signals that selling pressure may be weakening.

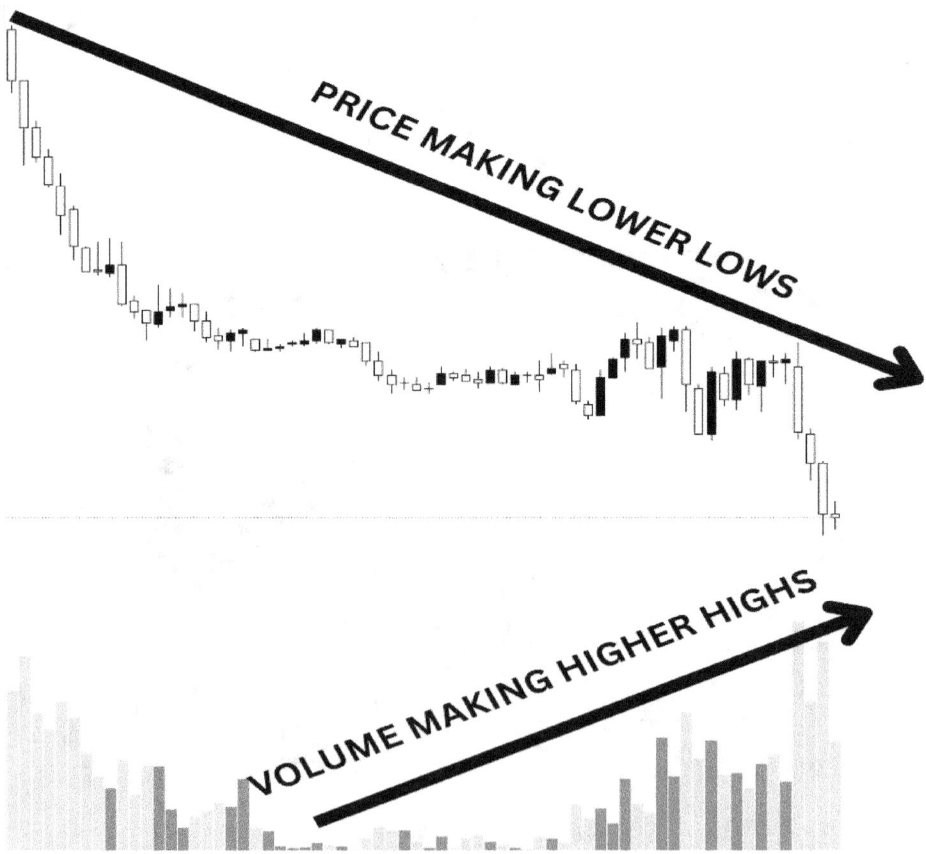

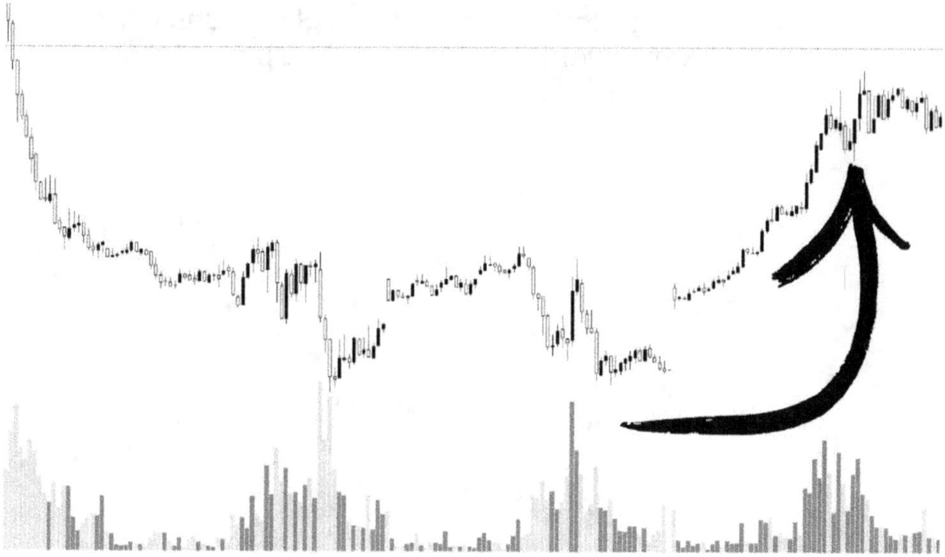

- **Bearish divergence:** Price makes higher highs while volume makes lower highs—suggests a potential exhaustion in buying interest.

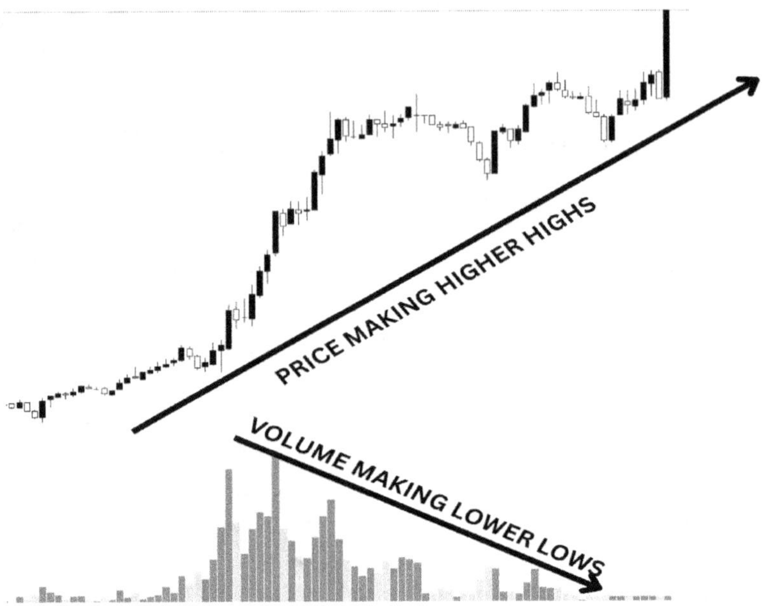

- When paired with moving average support/resistance, divergence becomes a **potent early signal** of trend shifts.

Volume-Based Moving Average Filters

- Use volume-based rules to **filter out weak trades**:
    - Only take moving average cross setups if volume is at least **20% above the 20-period average** volume.
    - Avoid entries if volume is declining on a breakout or trending move.
- Combine this approach with trend-following strategies for more reliable results.

Using Volume Weighted Moving Averages (VWMA)

- A VWMA is a moving average that gives more weight to periods with higher volume.
- It is ideal for scalpers and intraday traders who want to see **where most volume was traded** relative to price action.
- VWMA can help you:
    - Identify **fair value areas** for active price discovery.
    - Confirm breakouts by comparing price vs. VWMA position.
    - Avoid choppy, low-volume zones that often result in whipsaws.

Volume Spikes at Key Moving Average Levels

- Monitor for **volume spikes when price tests a moving average**:
    - If price bounces off the 200 EMA with increasing volume, it often signals institutional interest and a strong continuation move.

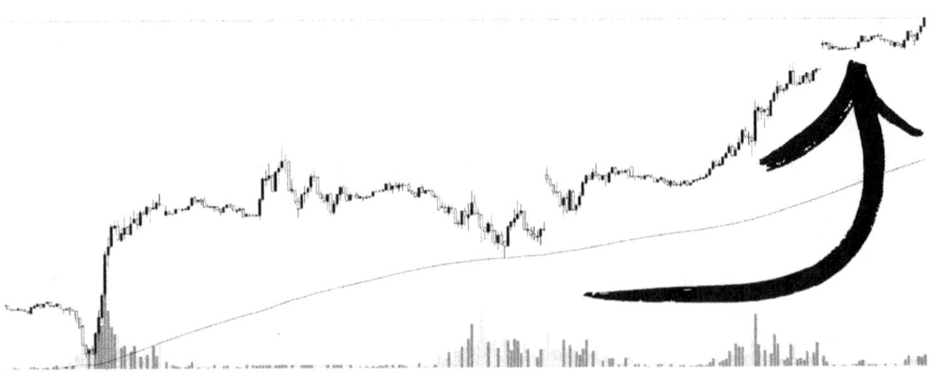

- A breakdown below a moving average with a volume surge may mark the beginning of a trend reversal.

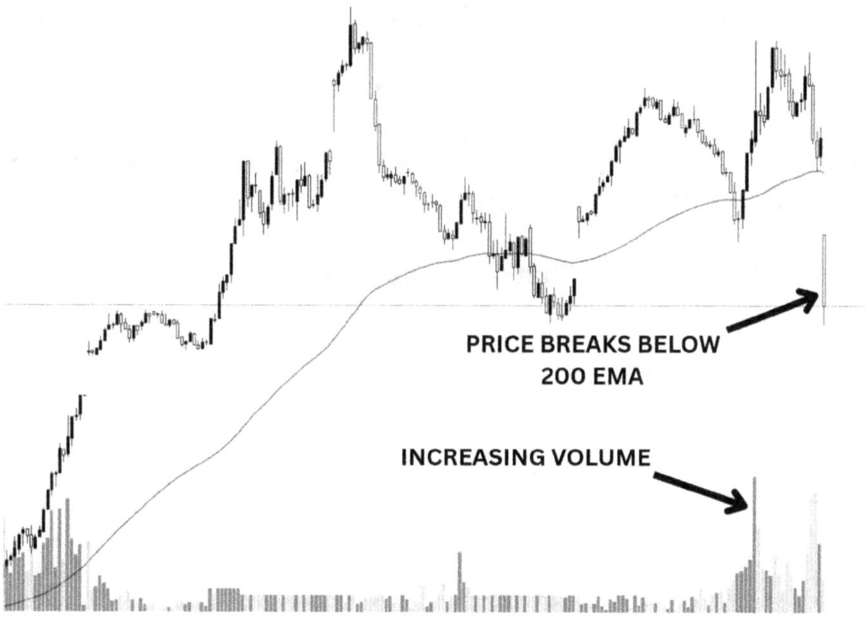

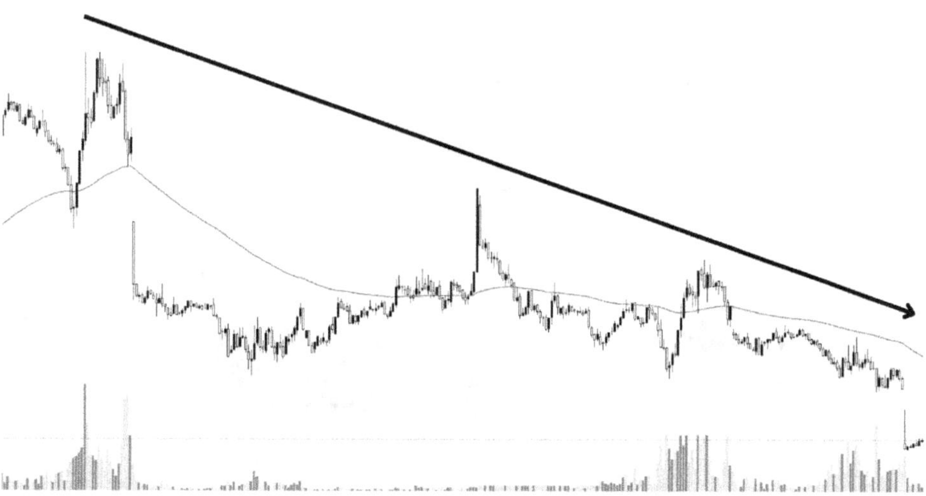

- Look for volume to **increase in the direction of the trend** after a moving average rejection to validate momentum.

Trade Example: Combining 20 EMA and Volume

- Let's say price pulls back to the 20 EMA in an uptrend.
- You wait for a bullish engulfing candle to form at the EMA.
- If that engulfing candle forms on **above-average volume**, it adds confidence to your trade.
- Without volume, that same candle may be weaker and prone to failure.

Best Volume Indicators to Pair with Moving Averages

- **Volume Moving Average:** A moving average applied to volume bars to detect breakouts in participation.

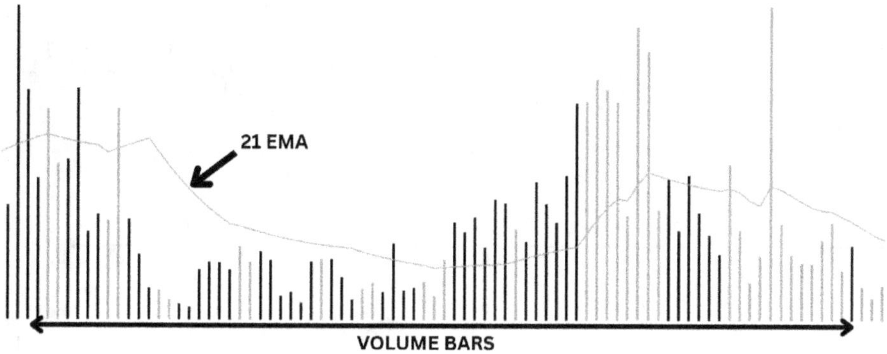

- **On-Balance Volume (OBV):** Measures cumulative buying and selling pressure.

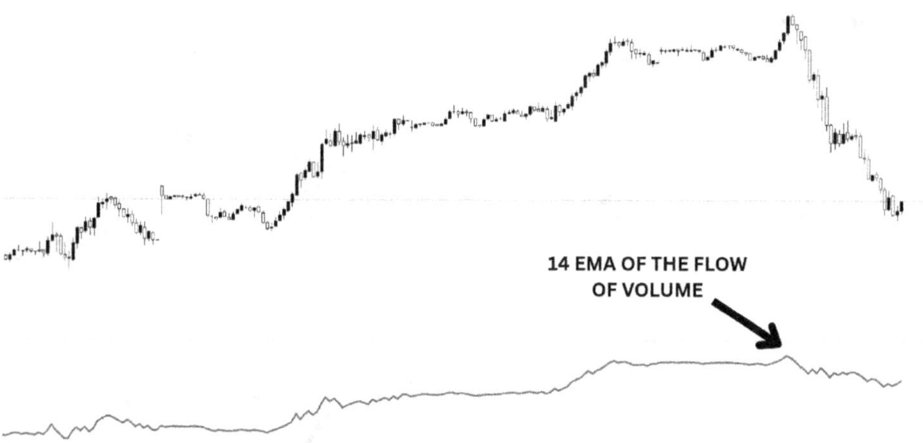

- **Volume Profile:** Shows the distribution of trading volume across different price levels, helping traders identify key support and resistance zones based on where the most buying and selling occurred.

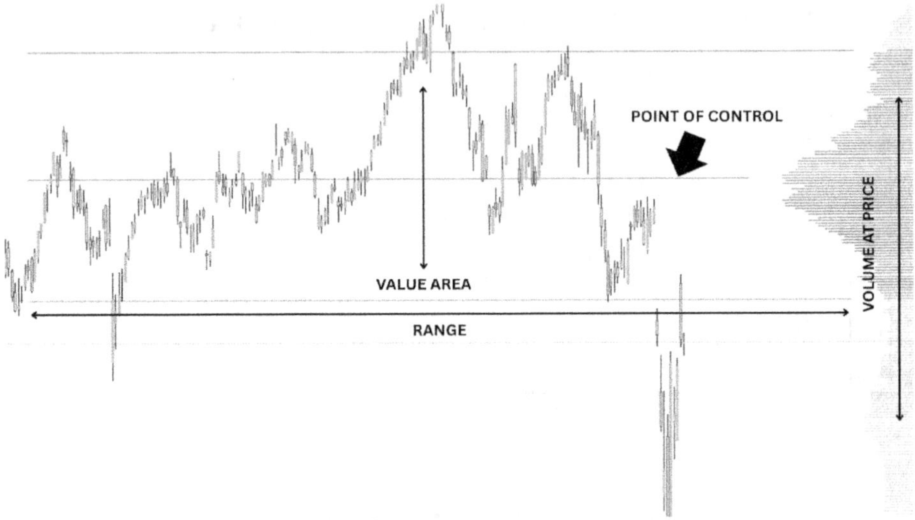

- **Volume Oscillator:** Compares short-term volume to long-term volume to detect shifts in activity.

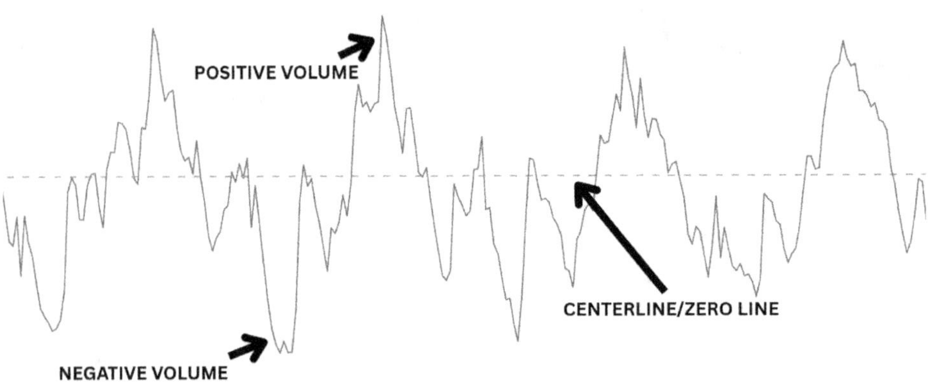

Summary

- Moving averages provide a trend framework, while volume reveals **strength and conviction** behind price movement.
- High volume during breakouts or bounces off moving averages increases the reliability of those signals.
- Using tools like VWMA, OBV, and volume divergence helps you fine-tune entries and avoid weak setups.

Key Takeaways

➢ Combining volume with moving averages gives your setups stronger confirmation and helps avoid false signals.

➢ Watch for volume spikes during moving average crossovers or retests to validate trend direction.

➢ Divergence between price and volume near moving averages often signals trend exhaustion or reversals.

➢ VWMA and other volume indicators can enhance your ability to identify institutional participation and trend strength.

➢ Use volume-based filters to avoid low-probability trades and increase your edge.

Chapter 8

Moving Averages and Market Cycles – Adapting Your Strategy to Market Phases

Introduction

Markets move in cycles—periods of expansion, contraction, accumulation, and distribution. Mastering moving averages means learning how to adapt them to each of these phases. A strategy that works beautifully in a trending market may fail in a range-bound one, and vice versa. In this chapter, you'll learn how to adjust your moving average approach to fit the broader market cycle you're trading in.

Understanding Market Cycles

- Market cycles reflect the psychology of participants over time—ranging from greed to fear.
- Each cycle is composed of **four main phases**:
    - **Accumulation:** Institutions and smart money begin buying quietly after a downturn.
    - **Uptrend (Expansion):** Prices begin trending upward as momentum builds.
    - **Distribution:** Price consolidates at highs while larger players begin to exit.
    - **Downtrend (Contraction):** Supply outweighs demand, leading to a decline.

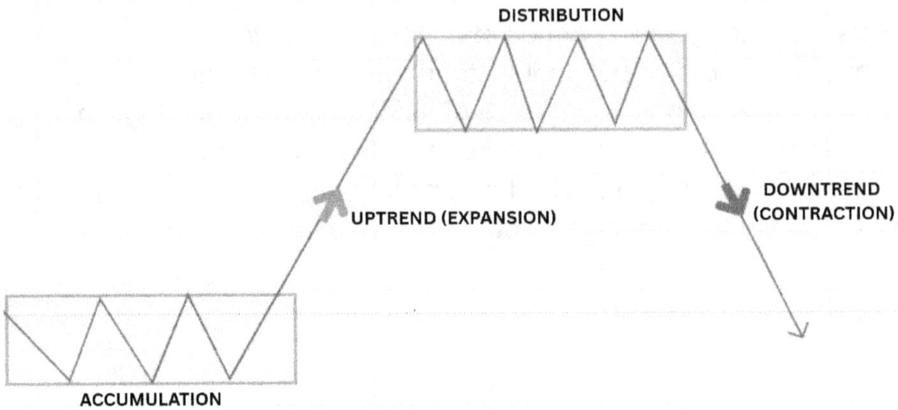

- Recognizing which phase you're in helps determine how to use moving averages effectively.

Using Moving Averages in the Accumulation Phase

- Price often moves sideways after a downtrend as large traders slowly accumulate positions.
- **Shorter-term moving averages** (e.g., 9 EMA or 20 SMA) can help identify the start of a shift.
- Look for:
    - Price crossing above the short-term MA with volume confirmation.
    - A flattening of the longer-term MA, like the 50 SMA or 100 EMA.
- Avoid using aggressive trend-following strategies until a clear breakout forms.

Moving Averages During Uptrends (Expansion Phase)

- This is where moving averages thrive. Trends are clean, and momentum is sustained.
- Key strategies:
    - Use the **9 EMA or 20 EMA** for pullback entries.
    - The **50 EMA** acts as a dynamic support for swing trading.
    - Look for stacked moving averages (short above medium above long) to confirm strength.
- Volume should support the price advance when price bounces off an MA.

Using Moving Averages in the Distribution Phase

- Distribution is characterized by sideways price action at elevated levels.
- Moving averages begin to **flatten out** and **converge**, reflecting indecision.
- Key signals:
    - Price begins crossing back and forth over short-term MAs without direction.
    - Watch for **bearish crossovers**, such as the 9 EMA crossing below the 20 EMA.
    - Use moving averages in conjunction with volume divergence and momentum indicators to spot fading strength.
- Trend strategies are less effective here—prepare to shift to breakout or reversion setups.

Navigating the Downtrend (Contraction Phase)

- In downtrends, moving averages become resistance rather than support.
- Look for:
    - Lower highs beneath a downward-sloping 20 EMA.
    - Short setups at the 9 EMA after a retracement.
    - Confirm with decreasing volume on rallies and increasing volume on drops.
- The **200 EMA or 100 SMA** can signal major resistance zones in prolonged downtrends.

Switching MA Settings Based on Market Conditions

- During strong trends:
  - **Shorter MAs** (like 9 EMA or 13 EMA) can help you stay closely aligned with momentum.

- During range-bound conditions:
  - **Longer MAs** (like 50 SMA or 100 SMA) help smooth out noise and provide better breakout signals.

- Tip: Create a **dynamic MA template** with three different lengths so you can adjust visually:
  - Fast (e.g., 9 EMA)
  - Medium (e.g., 21 EMA)
  - Slow (e.g., 50 or 100 EMA)

Combining MA with Cycle Recognition Tools

- Use **MACD**, **Stochastic**, or **RSI** to gauge cycle shifts alongside moving averages.
- **Volume analysis** helps confirm whether a phase shift is real or a fakeout.
- **Price structure** (higher highs and lows vs. lower highs and lows) should always be considered with your MAs.

Adapting Entry & Exit Rules to Market Cycles

- In uptrends: Use pullback entries to rising MAs with tight stop-losses.
- In sideways markets: Wait for clean breakouts above converging MAs.
- In downtrends: Enter on bounces to falling MAs; place stops above the recent swing high.
- Always adjust your **risk management** and **profit targets** based on volatility and market phase.

Summary

- Moving averages react differently in each market cycle phase.
- Learning to spot accumulation, expansion, distribution, and contraction phases allows you to adapt your strategy to current conditions.
- Fast-moving averages excel in strong trends, while slower ones filter noise during choppy or uncertain markets.

Key Takeaways

➢ Markets move in cycles—each phase requires a different use of moving averages.

➢ In accumulation, wait for moving average flattening and breakouts to confirm trend shifts.

➢ During trends, use short EMAs for entries and longer SMAs as dynamic support/resistance.

➢ Distribution phases cause MAs to converge and signal upcoming reversals.

➢ Downtrends flip MAs into resistance zones, ideal for shorting retracements.

➢ Always align your moving average strategy with the current market context for best results.

Chapter 9

Time of Day Analysis with Moving Averages – Mastering Market Rhythms

Introduction

Understanding how markets behave at different times of the trading day can give traders a powerful edge—especially when combined with moving averages. Futures markets are influenced by a global schedule, reacting to overlapping trading sessions, scheduled economic events, institutional activity, and periods of high or low liquidity. In this chapter, you'll learn how to apply time-of-day analysis across key futures markets—such as oil, gold, and index futures—using moving averages to time entries and exits with precision.

The Importance of Time-Based Market Behavior

- Every futures market has recurring behavioral patterns based on the time of day.
- Institutional activity, news releases, and global session overlaps can cause sharp volatility spikes.
- Moving averages help contextualize these intraday patterns, smoothing out noise and confirming direction within specific time windows.

Key Time Zones in Futures Trading

- **Pre-Market (7:00 AM – 9:30 AM ET):**
  - U.S. futures markets react to overnight developments in Europe and Asia.
  - Sharp moves are common in oil and gold as traders position themselves ahead of U.S. data releases.
  - Watch for moving average crossovers during pre-market range expansions.

- **Market Open (9:30 AM – 10:30 AM ET):**
  - Highest volume and volatility of the day.
  - Index futures like the S&P 500 (ES) tend to establish directional bias within the first hour.
  - Use short-term moving averages (e.g., 9-EMA, 20-EMA) to confirm breakout momentum or early mean reversion setups.

- **Midday (11:00 AM – 1:30 PM ET):**
    - Market often consolidates as institutional activity slows.
    - Ideal time for mean reversion trades in gold and oil.
    - Longer MAs like the 50-SMA can help you identify consolidating support and resistance zones.

- **Afternoon Session (1:30 PM – 3:30 PM ET):**
    - Institutional traders reposition for the close.
    - Watch for false breakouts and trend reversals.
    - Pair volume spikes with moving average slope shifts to confirm new directional moves.

- **Power Hour (3:30 PM – 4:00 PM ET):**
    - Final trading burst before the stock market close.
    - Great for breakout or breakdown trades on ES futures.
    - Shorter MAs respond faster to directional surges—avoid long-period MAs during this window.

- **After Hours (4:00 PM – 6:00 PM ET):**
    - Lower liquidity and thinner volume.
    - Gold and oil may still react to late-breaking geopolitical news.
    - Moving averages become less reliable due to lack of volume; tread cautiously.

Applying Time-of-Day Analysis to Specific Markets

Oil Futures (CL)

- Spikes often occur at 9:00 AM and 10:30 AM (when EIA inventory reports are released on Wednesdays).
- Early morning moves can be strong trend setups—use the 20-EMA and 50-SMA to confirm pullbacks.
- Afternoon chop is common unless driven by news—wait for clean MA convergence before entering.

Gold Futures (GC)

- Moves sharply on pre-market economic data and during European sessions (starting around 3:00 AM ET).
- Often mean reverts in late morning or midday; ideal for Bollinger Bands or VWAP combined with a 100-SMA.
- Moving averages flatten during slow periods—avoid trading if price stalls between MAs.

Index Futures (ES, NQ, YM)

- Respond aggressively to U.S. market open (9:30 AM ET).
- Directional bias established early—look for golden crosses (fast MA crossing above slow MA) around 10:00 AM.
- Afternoon reversals are common—watch the 15-EMA for sharp intraday fades or surges.

Choosing the Right Moving Averages for Different Times

- **Early Session (Pre-Market & Open):**
  - 9-EMA and 21-EMA are effective for spotting fast breakouts.

- **Midday:**
  - 50-SMA and 100-SMA work best for trend identification and range support/resistance.

- **Afternoon & Close:**
  - Pair short-term EMAs with VWAP for sharp directional moves.

- **Full-Day Context:**
  - Use 200-SMA to determine overall market trend and confluence zones.

Strategies for Different Time Windows

- **Opening Range Breakout Strategy (9:30–10:00 AM):**
    - Define the high and low of the first 30 minutes.
    - Use 9-EMA breakout confirmation and ride trend until 10:30–11:00 AM.

- **Midday Fade Strategy (11:00 AM–1:30 PM):**
    - Fade moves that are extended far above or below the 50-SMA.
    - Look for RSI divergences and a flattening slope on the MA.

- **Afternoon Reversal Strategy (2:00–3:30 PM):**
    - Monitor higher time frame MAs (e.g., 100-SMA on the 15-minute chart).
    - When price deviates and volume returns, anticipate a move back toward the MA.

Summary

- Time-of-day patterns influence futures market behavior more than most traders realize.
- Moving averages help traders recognize these intraday shifts in momentum and adapt strategy accordingly.
- Different futures markets—oil, gold, and equity indices—each have their own daily rhythm.
- Tailoring your moving average setups and strategies to match these time-based behaviors can significantly boost your accuracy and timing.

Key Takeaways

➢ Futures markets behave differently depending on the time of day—align your strategy accordingly.

➢ Use fast-moving averages (like 9-EMA) in high-volatility windows (e.g., market open).

➢ Use slower moving averages (like 50-SMA or 100-SMA) to trade mid-day consolidations or trend fades.

➢ Oil, gold, and index futures each have unique time-of-day characteristics—master them individually.

➢ Combine time-of-day context with moving average crossovers, volume, and price action for maximum edge.

Chapter 10

Moving Average Divergence – Spotting Imbalance Before Price Moves

Introduction

In this chapter, we dive into the concept of **Moving Average Divergence**—a powerful but underutilized method for anticipating momentum shifts, early reversals, and hidden strength or weakness in futures markets. While traders often focus on the price crossing a moving average, the *space between* moving averages (their divergence) can offer clues about underlying market dynamics **before** price makes a significant move.

This approach is especially useful for traders in **oil, gold, and index futures**, where institutional behavior and volume imbalances often precede price changes.

What Is Moving Average Divergence?

- Moving Average Divergence refers to the *widening or narrowing distance* between two or more moving averages.
- This technique focuses not on crossovers themselves, but on the *rate and angle of separation or convergence* between the averages.
- It reveals **momentum strength**, **volatility contraction**, and potential **trend exhaustion**.

Why Divergence Matters More Than Crossovers

- Crossovers often occur **after** a move has already started. Divergence, on the other hand, can *warn you ahead of time*.
- Divergence reveals whether a trend is **gaining power** (moving averages accelerating away from each other) or **losing steam** (moving averages tightening or converging).
- It adds a **third dimension** to your moving average analysis: not just where price is, but how *velocity and separation* are evolving.

How to Measure Divergence Effectively

- Use **two moving averages**: a short-term (e.g., 9 EMA) and a longer-term (e.g., 21 EMA or 50 EMA).
- Track the **distance between the two lines** on your chart:
    - If the distance is expanding and price is moving in the trend's direction → **momentum is strong**.

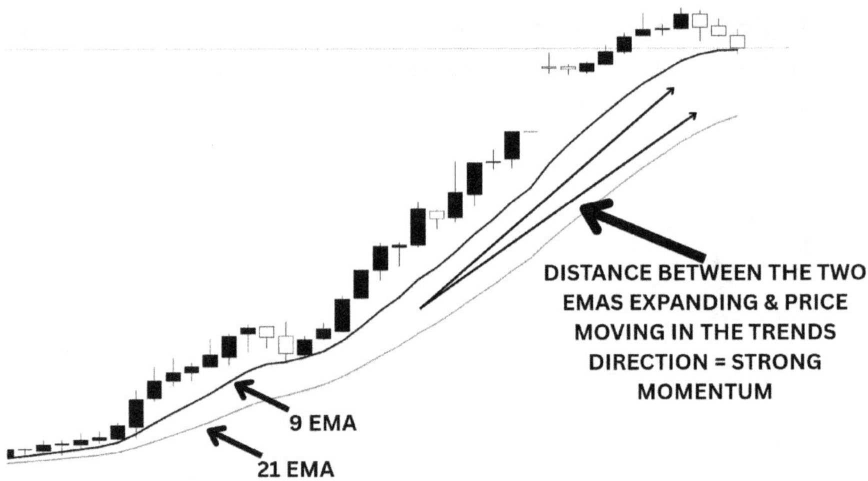

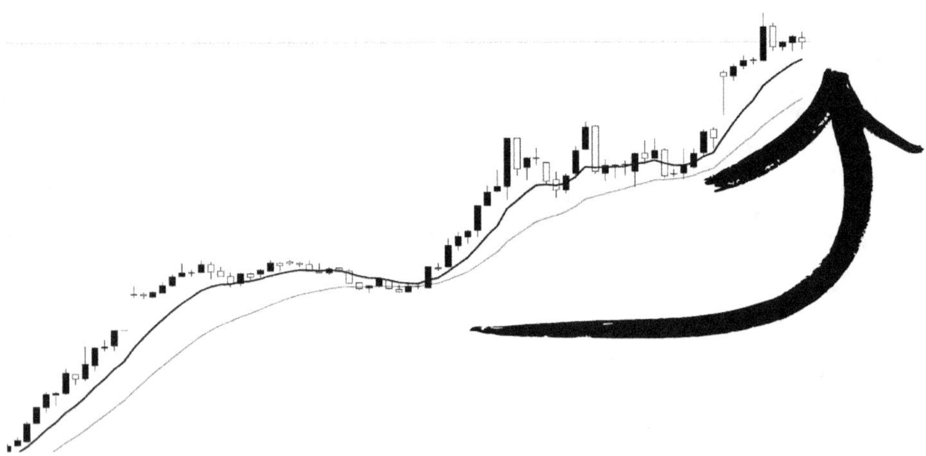

- If the distance is shrinking while price still moves → **momentum is weakening**, possible reversal coming.

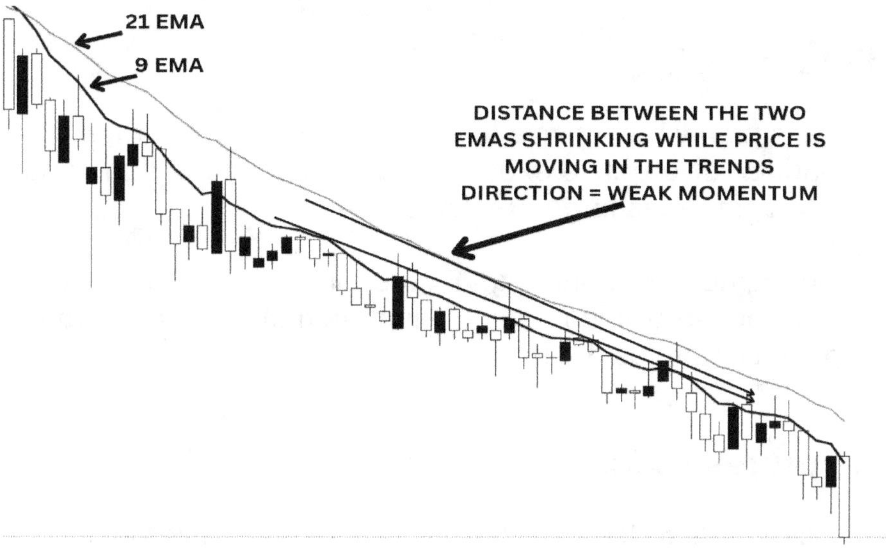

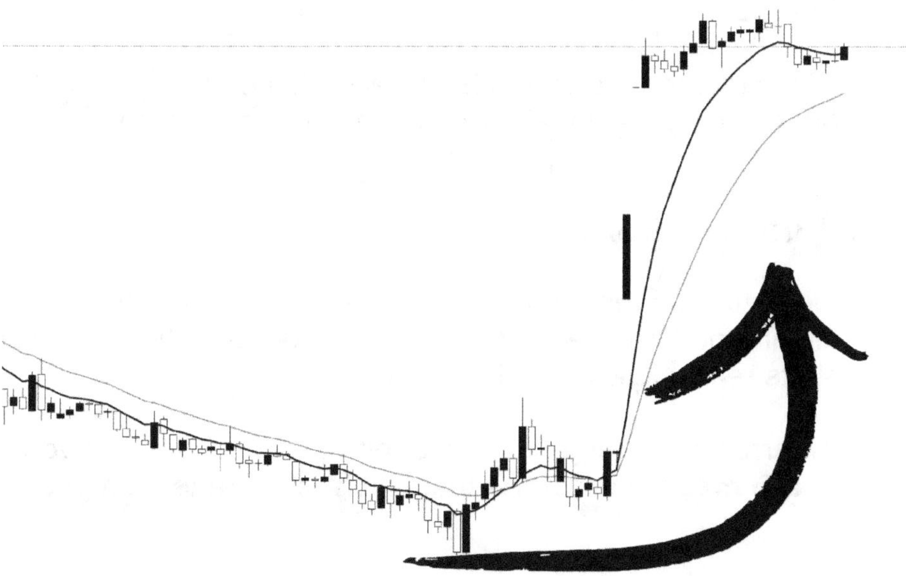

- Watch for **flattening of one or both lines**. If the short MA flattens first, it often signals a pullback is near.

Applications in Oil, Gold, and Index Futures

Oil Futures (CL):

- Oil is highly responsive to institutional volume surges. Sudden divergence expansion after a period of tight range often precedes large breakouts.
- During news events (e.g., EIA reports), divergence can explode—providing early confirmation of direction before price completes the move.

Gold Futures (GC):

- Gold tends to trend smoothly. Watching for divergence tightening in an uptrend often signals **distribution** or **buyer fatigue**.
- When divergence expands on low volume, it may indicate **false strength**—ideal for fading moves at resistance.

Index Futures (ES/NQ):

- Index futures respond heavily to order flow and trend alignment. Divergence patterns often develop *before* major shifts (e.g., FOMC or CPI days).
- A narrowing divergence in a strong trend can foreshadow **sharp mean reversions** that catch retail traders off guard.

Three Powerful Divergence Setups

- **Squeeze Divergence Setup:**
    - Look for long periods where MAs stay tight (squeezed).
    - As price compresses and divergence narrows, a sudden *burst* in divergence usually marks breakout direction.

- **Reversal Divergence Setup:**
    - In strong trends, if price continues upward but divergence narrows → early warning of trend exhaustion.
    - Combine with RSI or MACD for even better accuracy.

- **Fakeout Filter:**
    - If price breaks a key level but divergence does not expand → likely a fakeout.
    - Use divergence confirmation to avoid being trapped.

Combining Divergence with Volume and Candle Patterns

- Add **volume spikes** as confirmation. Divergence expansion plus surging volume = high-probability breakout.
- Watch for **candle signals** (e.g., hammers, engulfing) at the moment divergence begins expanding or contracting—these reinforce your setup.

Summary

- Moving Average Divergence is the study of *space and speed* between moving averages rather than just crossover points.
- Widening divergence suggests **strong trend momentum**, while tightening divergence suggests **potential reversal or consolidation**.
- This technique adds predictive power and helps futures traders catch early entries and avoid late ones, especially in volatile markets like oil, gold, and indices.

Key Takeaways

➤ Moving Average Divergence helps you detect trend strength and weakness before price confirms a move.

➤ Expanding divergence signals strong momentum; contracting divergence often signals exhaustion or consolidation.

➤ Divergence is especially powerful when combined with volume and candle confirmation signals.

➤ Oil, gold, and index futures all respond reliably to divergence patterns, particularly around news events and high-volume sessions.

➤ Use divergence to improve timing, filter out fakeouts, and increase the reliability of breakout and reversal setups.

Chapter 11

The Psychology Behind Moving Average Respect – Why Price Reacts to MAs

Introduction

While moving averages are mathematical tools, their true power lies in how humans interact with them. Traders across all levels—from beginners to institutions—watch moving averages like the 20, 50, or 200 on every chart. But why does price so often "respect" them? Why do reversals, bounces, and even trends form around these simple lines?

In this chapter, we'll explore the **psychological mechanics** behind price reacting to moving averages. By understanding crowd behavior and the invisible consensus that forms around MAs, you can trade them with greater precision and confidence.

Moving Averages as Self-Fulfilling Prophecies

- Moving averages work not because of their inherent magic, but because *everyone is watching them*.
- The more eyes on an average (like the 50 or 200), the more likely it is that traders will place buy/sell orders around it.
- This creates a feedback loop where price respects the MA—not because of the line itself, but because of the **mass behavior** it inspires.

Support, Resistance, and Trader Memory

- MAs often act as dynamic support and resistance because traders **remember** how price behaved near them in the past.
- When price bounces from the 50 EMA on oil futures multiple times, traders begin to trust it as a key level.
- This "anchored memory" causes market participants to act **predictably**, reinforcing the level's power.

Institutional Use of Moving Averages

- Institutions use large MAs (like the 100 and 200 SMA) to assess long-term positioning.
- When institutional algorithms buy near the 200 SMA on S&P 500 futures, it creates massive volume and reaction.
- Smart money often enters or scales out near these levels—not to respect the average, but to exploit the reaction others will have to it.

The Herd Mentality Around MAs

- Herd behavior explains why a moving average bounce can occur even when fundamentals don't support it.
- Traders prefer *following others*—especially around clear, simple signals like a moving average touch or crossover.
- This creates **momentum surges**, where new orders come in because of collective confirmation, not individual conviction.

How Fear and Greed Shape Reactions Around MAs

- When price approaches a well-watched MA from above, fear of losing profits often causes early selling.
- When price drops to an MA from below, hope or greed can cause aggressive buying in anticipation of a bounce.
- Understanding these emotions helps you read the crowd and enter *before* the majority acts.

Psychological Anchors: Why Specific MAs Matter More

- Certain numbers have psychological weight (20, 50, 100, 200), creating a kind of numeric comfort zone.
- These levels are taught in textbooks, trading courses, and used in algorithms.
- The psychological repetition of these MAs across platforms and timeframes reinforces their power.

How Belief Reinforces Reaction Patterns

- If traders *believe* a bounce will occur at the 21 EMA on the 1-hour gold chart, they'll trade accordingly.
- That belief results in real market orders, which in turn *makes* the bounce happen.
- Belief becomes behavior, and behavior becomes price movement.

Anticipation vs. Reaction: Timing the Crowd

- Experienced traders often enter slightly before the MA is touched, anticipating a crowd reaction.
- Less experienced traders wait for confirmation and enter late—right before the MA fails.
- Knowing how traders *typically* react gives you an edge in deciding whether to front-run or fade the reaction.

Case Studies by Market: Psychological Patterns

Oil Futures (CL)

- Retail traders tend to pile in at the 21 EMA due to its frequent use on lower timeframes.
- Institutional players often wait until the 50 EMA or VWAP aligns before entering heavy size.

Gold Futures (GC)

- Gold often respects the 200 SMA on daily charts due to central bank and long-horizon investor attention.
- Quick-moving EMAs (like 9 or 13) are used by scalpers to catch temporary sentiment reversals.

S&P 500 Futures (ES)

- The 50 and 200 SMAs are watched on all timeframes, making them ideal for swing and position traders.
- Emotional reactions (panic buying/selling) often occur when these levels break or hold dramatically.

Summary

The reason moving averages “work” isn’t just due to mathematical formulas—it’s due to the predictable **psychological behavior** they trigger. From herd mentality and emotional anchors to institutional footprints and trader memory, moving averages are tools of mass psychology. Recognizing how other traders react to them lets you get ahead of the curve and build smarter, more strategic trades.

Key Takeaways

➢ Price respects moving averages primarily because they are widely observed and acted upon by traders.

➢ Support/resistance behavior around MAs is often driven by collective memory and crowd expectations.

➢ Institutional traders use MAs strategically to exploit retail behavior, not just as signals.

➢ Emotions like fear and greed drive behavior around MAs, often leading to predictable price reactions.

➢ Understanding mass psychology around specific MAs can help you anticipate reactions before they happen.

➢ Belief in the MA's power leads to real order flow, which reinforces the effectiveness of the MA.

➢ Every market (oil, gold, S&P 500) has unique psychological behaviors tied to different moving averages.

Chapter 12

Moving Averages and Liquidity Zones – Identifying Smart Money Activity

Introduction

Moving averages are powerful tools on their own, but when combined with liquidity zones, they reveal something even more valuable: **where the smart money is likely to act**. In this chapter, we explore how moving averages often overlap with high-liquidity areas—zones where large players quietly enter or exit positions—giving retail traders a unique edge.

Understanding the intersection between **moving averages and liquidity** helps you spot institutional footprints, avoid traps, and enter positions with precision. Let's dive into how to align these tools to identify high-probability setups in futures markets.

What Are Liquidity Zones?

- Liquidity zones are price areas where high trade volume occurs, typically because many traders are active there.
- These zones attract large institutional orders because they provide the ability to enter or exit large positions without moving the market too much.
- Liquidity zones often appear at:
    - Key swing highs and lows
    - Consolidation ranges
    - Breakout or breakdown levels
    - Well-watched moving averages (like the 50 or 200 SMA/EMA)

Why Institutions Gravitate Toward Moving Averages

- Institutions avoid entering the market with visible market orders—they rely on **liquidity** to mask their size.
- Popular moving averages often coincide with high-volume areas, which provide institutions the cover to place massive orders.
- For example, when price retraces to the 50 EMA on a 1-hour oil chart after a breakout, institutions may absorb retail sell orders to go long.

Moving Averages as Dynamic Liquidity Anchors

- Unlike static support/resistance levels, moving averages evolve with price, acting as **dynamic liquidity magnets**.
- Traders cluster orders around popular MAs (like the 21, 50, or 200), increasing the odds of large activity when price touches these levels.
- As price approaches the MA:
  - Retail traders place stop orders nearby
  - Institutions may target these levels to absorb liquidity or trigger stop hunts

Identifying Liquidity Traps Around MAs

- **Liquidity traps** occur when institutions lure traders into obvious setups—then reverse the price.
- Common example: A bullish bounce off the 50 EMA pulls in buyers, only to reverse sharply as institutions use the surge in volume to sell.
- MAs can act as bait when combined with retail sentiment, particularly after emotional candles or news events.

Overlaying Volume Profile with Moving Averages

- Using **Volume Profile** alongside MAs helps confirm if a moving average aligns with a high-volume node (liquidity pocket).
- When an MA lines up with a Point of Control (POC) or high-volume area, it becomes a **high-value area** for potential entry.

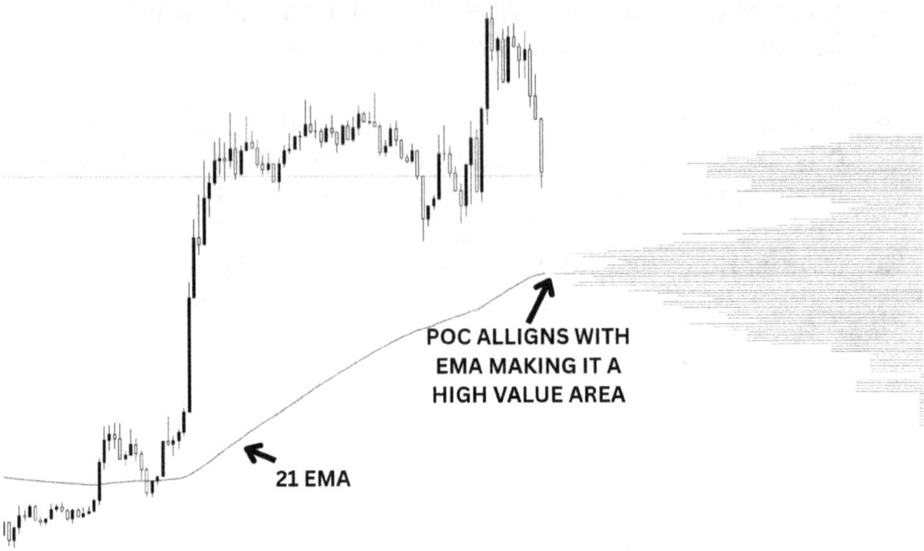

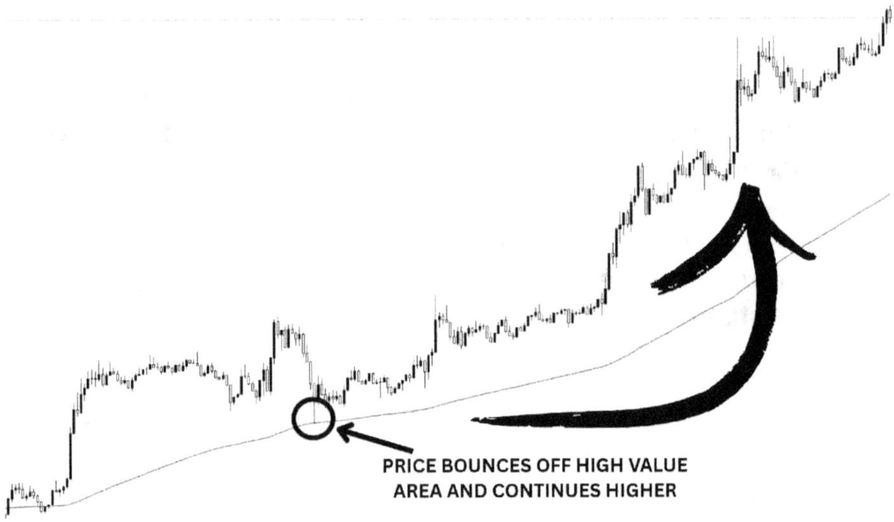

- These overlaps are prime zones for reversals or strong continuations.

Timeframes and Liquidity Behavior

- **Shorter timeframes (1m–15m)**: Liquidity often clusters around the VWAP and 21 EMA.
- **Medium timeframes (1h–4h)**: Watch for 50 and 100 EMAs, often used by intraday swing traders and algo systems.
- **Higher timeframes (Daily–Weekly)**: The 200 SMA becomes a long-term magnet for smart money positioning and portfolio rebalancing.

Examples by Market: Liquidity and MA Alignment

Oil Futures (CL)

- The 21 EMA often attracts large scalper volume.
- Institutional entries tend to occur around the 50 EMA or VWAP re-tests after aggressive directional moves.

Gold Futures (GC)

- Smart money frequently uses the 200 SMA on the daily chart as a reloading point during major trend phases.
- Price often stalls or sharply reverses when it converges with high-volume zones and key MAs.

S&P 500 Futures (ES)

- The 50 and 100 EMAs on the 1-hour and 4-hour charts frequently act as re-entry zones for institutional trend continuation trades.
- Heavy volume often appears when these MAs align with prior consolidation or breakout levels.

Using Liquidity and MAs to Plan Traps and Exits

- Instead of chasing breakouts, use MA-liquidity overlaps as **entry pullback points** when volume spikes.
- Exit partials when price approaches a major MA that coincides with a previous value area.
- Watch for **liquidity sweeps** (stop hunts) near MAs, especially during economic news events—these are smart money manipulation tactics.

How to Confirm Smart Money Activity Near MAs

- Look for:
    - Sudden volume spikes with small price movement (absorption)
    - Wicky candles or dojis around key MAs
    - Reversals following price running into a liquidity pocket + MA alignment
- Use order flow tools or cumulative delta (if available) to spot aggressive absorption or hidden buyers/sellers

Summary

Moving averages aren't just technical tools—they are *behavioral magnets* for volume and institutional activity. When they align with liquidity zones, they become even more powerful. By learning to recognize where smart money is likely to operate, you can anticipate moves, spot traps, and structure trades with greater confidence.

Key Takeaways

➢ Liquidity zones are high-volume areas where institutions can enter/exit without slippage—often aligning with moving averages.

➢ Moving averages serve as dynamic magnets for order flow, drawing in retail traders and institutions alike.

➢ Smart money often enters or exits near MAs when they align with high-volume nodes or prior market structure.

➢ MAs can act as bait in liquidity traps—leading to stop hunts and rapid reversals.

➢ Combining moving averages with volume profile or order flow tools helps confirm institutional footprints.

➢ Each market has unique MA-liquidity dynamics—understanding these gives you a major strategic edge.

➢ Watching for MA + liquidity overlap helps you plan high-probability entries, exits, and avoid emotional trades.

Chapter 13

Custom Timeframe Blending – Building Hybrid MAs from Multiple Timeframes

Introduction

One of the biggest breakthroughs a trader can make is learning to think **multi-dimensionally**. While most traders use moving averages on individual charts, advanced traders begin to blend timeframes—merging signals from different intervals into a single, custom view. This technique, called **timeframe blending**, can be used to build hybrid moving averages that reveal deeper market rhythm and smart money positioning.

In this chapter, we'll explore how to design and apply **custom blended moving averages**—those that combine multiple timeframes into a singular dynamic guide for timing entries, exits, and trade filters. Whether you scalp oil futures on the 1-minute chart or swing trade S&P 500 futures on the 4-hour, hybrid MAs can elevate your clarity and consistency.

What Is Timeframe Blending?

- Timeframe blending is the practice of integrating data from multiple timeframes into a single analytical tool—such as a customized moving average.

- Rather than switching between charts, traders can build **hybrid MAs** that pull higher timeframe logic into a lower timeframe view.

- The goal is to **synchronize** with institutional flows that operate across multiple timeframes simultaneously.

Why Use Custom Hybrid MAs?

- Moving averages from higher timeframes often **act as invisible support/resistance** on lower timeframes.
- Hybrid MAs help traders anticipate reactions at these hidden zones without constantly switching charts.
- They also help filter noise and false signals by aligning trends and key zones across multiple perspectives.

How to Build Custom Blended MAs

There are several ways to create hybrid moving averages using multiple timeframes:

1. Weighted Average of MAs from Multiple Charts

- Calculate the 21 EMA from the 15-minute, 1-hour, and 4-hour timeframes.
- Combine them using weights (e.g., 50% from the current TF, 30% from 1 TF above, 20% from 2 TFs above).
- Plot the weighted result as a **custom overlay** on your main chart.

2. Overlay Higher TF MAs on Lower Charts

- On platforms like TradingView or NinjaTrader, overlay higher-timeframe MAs (e.g., Daily 200 EMA) directly on your intraday chart.

- This helps spot when price is reacting to a higher-level average even while trading in a lower timeframe.

3. Use Multi-Timeframe Indicators or Scripts

- Create a script that calculates the average of multiple MAs across different timeframes and outputs a single value.
- Example: A script that takes the 50 EMA from the 1-hour chart and the 100 EMA from the 4-hour chart, then averages them to create a hybrid support zone.

Best MA Combinations for Hybrid Use

For Scalping:

- Combine 9 EMA (1m), 21 EMA (5m), and 50 EMA (15m) into one hybrid MA.
- This helps align micro-trend momentum with short-term institutional flows.

For Intraday Swing Trading:

- Blend the 21 EMA (15m), 50 EMA (1h), and 100 EMA (4h).
- Useful in markets like S&P 500 futures (ES) or oil (CL) for trend alignment.

For Position Trading:

- Mix the 100 EMA (4h), 200 EMA (Daily), and 50 EMA (Weekly).
- Helps swing traders in gold (GC) or other high-volatility instruments spot long-term inflection zones.

Reading Price Action Against Hybrid MAs

- When price **bounces cleanly** off a hybrid MA, it signals a strong confluence of timeframes.
- **Wicks or rejections** from hybrid MAs suggest institutional defense of trend zones.
- If price **consolidates around** a blended MA, it may indicate indecision or an upcoming high-impact move.

Filtering Trades with Custom MAs

- Only trade in the direction of your hybrid MA slope for trend-following setups.
- Use hybrid MAs as confirmation layers—e.g., if price breaks above the 21 EMA but still sits below the hybrid MA, avoid long entries.
- In range conditions, the hybrid MA can act as a **mid-range mean** for mean reversion plays.

Challenges and Tips for Using Hybrid MAs

- **Data lag**: Hybrid MAs that use higher timeframe data will update less frequently.
- **Backtesting complexity**: These MAs require more custom coding or careful manual testing.
- **Visual clutter**: Avoid overlaying too many lines—use color or opacity to simplify.

Pro tip: Use a single line to represent your hybrid MA and label it clearly (e.g., "Multi-TF EMA"). Treat it like a dynamic S/R zone, not a static signal.

Summary

Custom blended moving averages unlock a powerful way to align your trading with multiple timeframes without having to jump between charts. These hybrid MAs act as convergence zones where trends, liquidity, and institutional order flow intersect. Whether you trade fast-paced markets like oil or long-cycle setups in gold or equities, timeframe blending helps you maintain clarity and avoid low-quality trades.

Key Takeaways

➤ Timeframe blending creates hybrid MAs by combining moving averages from different timeframes into a single line of confluence.

➤ Hybrid MAs act as powerful support/resistance zones, reflecting institutional order flow and trend alignment.

➤ Scalpers, intraday traders, and swing traders can each customize their MA blends based on their strategy and timeframe.

➤ Platforms like TradingView, NinjaTrader, or custom scripts allow you to overlay or combine multiple timeframe MAs visually.

➤ Custom MAs help filter noise, enhance entry timing, and improve consistency by keeping your trades aligned with the broader trend.

Chapter 14

Invisible Moving Averages – How Institutions Use Non-Standard Periods

Introduction

Institutional traders don't always follow the rules retail traders are taught. While retail education often focuses on common moving average periods like the 9, 20, 50, 100, or 200, institutions frequently apply **non-standard moving average periods** that aren't widely known or visible. These *invisible moving averages* create levels of support and resistance that catch most traders off guard—causing sudden reversals, unexpected bounces, or confusing price stalls.

This chapter reveals how institutions use these tools to disguise their true intent, how you can identify these hidden levels, and how to integrate them into your strategy to track smart money footprints more effectively.

What Are Invisible Moving Averages?

- Invisible moving averages refer to **non-standard period MAs** that aren't commonly discussed in retail trading circles.

- Institutions often use custom timeframes (e.g., 13 EMA, 21 EMA, 34 EMA, 144 EMA, or 233 SMA) derived from Fibonacci sequences or proprietary models.

- These levels are *invisible* only in the sense that most traders don't have them plotted—yet price still reacts to them.

Why Institutions Use Non-Standard Periods

- **Avoid Crowd Clustering**: When everyone uses the same levels (e.g., the 50 or 200), those levels can become self-fulfilling. Institutions often prefer to *hide their tracks* by using unconventional averages.

- **Order Layering**: Algorithms may be set to layer orders around multiple custom averages to manage risk and scale into large positions stealthily.

- **Fibonacci Logic**: Many institutional models integrate Fibonacci periods (e.g., 13, 21, 34, 55, 89, 144) to track natural market rhythm and reversion zones.

- **Unique Timeframe Blending**: Large firms often use customized time compression models—e.g., combining the 15-min and 2-hour MA into a proprietary "blended" MA unique to their system.

Common Invisible Moving Averages and Their Origins

- **13 EMA / SMA** – A short-term Fibonacci-based average used for micro-trend signals.
- **21 EMA / SMA** – Frequently used in trending environments for pullback entries.
- **34 EMA** – Popular among institutional scalpers and swing traders for trend continuation confirmation.
- **89 or 144 EMA** – Higher timeframe institutional zones that act like a "soft 200" for complex trend structures.
- **233 SMA** – An institutional-level long-term average with roots in Fibonacci extensions.

How to Identify Invisible Moving Average Zones

- **Unexplained Reactions**: If price suddenly bounces or reverses without any visible indicator or support/resistance nearby, try overlaying custom MAs like the 13, 21, or 89 to test for alignment.
- **Volume Confluence**: Watch for increased volume or aggressive wick action at points that align with non-standard MAs.
- **Repeated Structure Reactions**: Backtest over 100+ charts to look for consistent reactions to the same uncommon moving average across multiple instruments and timeframes.

Practical Tools to Detect Hidden MA Influence

- **Overlay MAs You're Not Using**: Try adding 13, 21, 34, 89, 144, and 233 MAs on your charts—even if temporarily.
- **Multi-Timeframe Backtesting**: Look for times where these MAs align across intraday and higher timeframe charts to spot high-probability levels.
- **Volume Spike Filters**: When unusual MAs line up with high-volume candles or pivot reactions, it's a likely sign of institutional presence.

How to Use Invisible MAs to Your Advantage

- **Preemptive Entry Levels**: Use lesser-known MAs to anticipate pullbacks or trend continuation moves *before* price hits standard MAs that attract crowd activity.
- **Stop Placement Precision**: Use invisible MAs to place tighter, smarter stops in areas where institutions are likely to defend their positions.
- **Liquidity Fade Zones**: When retail traders get shaken out by sharp rejections or fakeouts, you can position ahead of them using these under-watched MAs.

Cross-Market Applications

This concept isn't limited to one asset class. Here's how it plays out across major markets:

- **Oil Futures (CL)**: Often respects the 21 and 89 EMAs on the 15-min and 1H charts, even when the 50 EMA shows no confluence.
- **Gold Futures (GC)**: The 144 EMA tends to mark long-term bounce zones on the 4H and daily charts.
- **Index Futures (ES/NQ)**: Short-term algorithms may react strongly to the 13 and 34 EMAs on 5-min and 15-min charts.
- **Currencies (6E, 6J)**: Highly reactive to 21/34 EMAs across both intraday and swing levels.

Summary

Invisible moving averages—non-standard, often Fibonacci-based periods—are powerful institutional tools used to hide large orders and create unexpected market reactions. Retail traders who learn to track and implement these hidden levels gain insight into smart money behavior and can anticipate price movements more accurately. By overlaying less-common MAs on your charts and watching for repeated reactions, you'll begin to uncover the silent fingerprints of institutional traders.

Key Takeaways

➢ Invisible moving averages are non-standard MA periods often used by institutions to hide their activity and avoid crowd behavior.

➢ Common examples include the 13, 21, 34, 89, 144, and 233 EMAs or SMAs—many of which are Fibonacci-derived.

➢ Price often reacts at these levels even when there are no standard support/resistance areas nearby.

➢ Traders can use these MAs for early entries, smarter stops, and fade setups against crowded retail zones.

➢ These hidden MAs work across oil, gold, index, and currency futures—especially on intraday and swing timeframes.

➢ Backtest and experiment with multi-timeframe overlays to identify which invisible MAs your market of choice respects most.

Chapter 15

Moving Averages in Range-Bound Markets – Surviving the Chop

Introduction

While trending markets offer clean signals and clear momentum, range-bound markets—commonly referred to as “choppy” or “sideways” conditions—present one of the greatest challenges for moving average users. In these environments, price often whipsaws above and below moving averages, generating false entries and stop-outs.

This chapter explores how to identify range-bound conditions early, adjust your moving average strategy accordingly, and use specific MA configurations to avoid getting chopped up. By understanding how MAs behave during consolidations, you can survive—and even profit—from these tricky environments.

Recognizing Range-Bound Conditions

- **Definition**: A range-bound market occurs when price moves horizontally within a confined zone, bouncing between support and resistance rather than trending up or down.

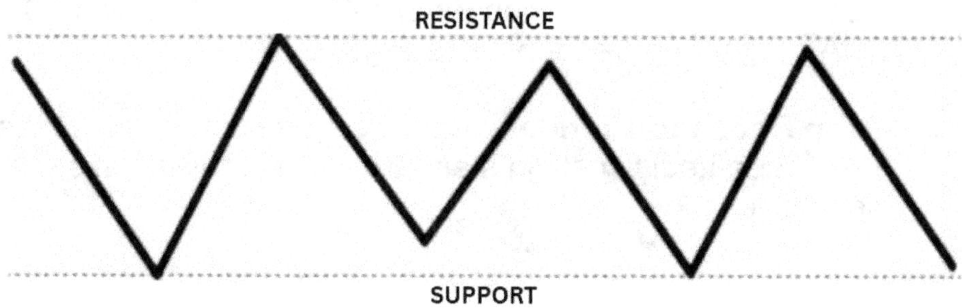

- **Visual Cues**:
  - Price repeatedly bounces between horizontal support and resistance.
  - Moving averages flatten or crisscross repeatedly.
  - Trend-following indicators (like ADX) drop below 20, signaling lack of direction.
- **Behavioral Shift**: Traders often enter trend trades too early during consolidation, only to be whipsawed repeatedly.

How Moving Averages Behave in Sideways Markets

- **Flattened Moving Averages**: In choppy conditions, most MAs—especially shorter-period ones like the 9 EMA or 20 EMA—flatten and offer little directional guidance.
- **Frequent Crossovers**: Fast-moving averages will often cross above and below longer ones (e.g., 9 EMA over 20 EMA), triggering frequent false signals.
- **Mean Reversion Tendencies**: Price gravitates back to the mean repeatedly, making standard trend-following systems ineffective.

Using MAs to Detect and Avoid Chop

- **MA Angle Filtering**:
    - Use slope filters—only take trades when the 20 or 50 EMA is clearly angled (not flat).
    - Set alerts for flattening slopes to pause entries.

- **MA Distance Compression**:
    - When multiple MAs (e.g., 9, 20, 50) converge tightly, it often signals consolidation.
    - Avoid new trades until the averages re-separate and trend resumes.

- **ADX with MAs**:
    - Combine moving averages with ADX. If ADX < 20 and MAs are flat, skip trend setups.
    - Resume trend trades only when ADX rises and MAs regain slope.

Best Moving Averages for Range Conditions

- **Volume-Weighted Moving Average (VWMA)**:
    - Reacts more accurately in low-momentum conditions by factoring volume.
    - Can serve as a “fair value” benchmark in choppy conditions.

- **Smoothed Moving Averages (e.g., Hull MA)**:
    - Reduces noise and avoids overreacting to minor swings within a range.

- **Envelope + MA Combinations**:
    - Envelopes around a central MA (like a 20 SMA ± 1.5%) help define upper and lower range boundaries.
    - Look for price rejection at the outer bands instead of traditional crossover signals.

Range Trading with MAs: Practical Strategies

- **Mean Reversion Entries**:
    - Fade price extensions away from a flat 20 or 50 EMA when range structure is confirmed.
    - Example: If price spikes above resistance but MAs are flat and ADX is low, consider shorting back to the mean.

- **Inside-Bar MA Fades**:
    - Combine inside-bar patterns with flat MA zones. These setups suggest range continuation.

- **Avoid Trend Breakouts**:
    - Avoid entering on moving average crossovers during consolidation. Wait for breakout confirmation *and* increasing slope.

Common Traps to Avoid in Chop

- **Trusting Crossovers Blindly**:
  - A 9/20 EMA crossover during a flat 50 EMA likely results in a whipsaw.

- **Ignoring Context**:
  - Always assess structure before acting on any MA signal. Flat MAs are a clue, not a trade trigger.

- **Overtrading**:
  - Choppy environments generate many signals—but few good trades. Be selective and patient.

Market Examples of Choppy MA Behavior

- **Oil Futures (CL)**: Known for sharp directional runs, but often reverts violently during range-bound days. The 34 EMA on the 15-min chart can act as a chop filter—flat slope means stand aside.
- **Gold Futures (GC)**: During sideways action, gold may oscillate cleanly between a flat 20 and 50 EMA—providing short-term mean reversion setups.
- **S&P 500 Futures (ES)**: In pre-market or midday sessions, price often hugs the VWAP and 9 EMA. These can act as dynamic range centers during low volatility periods.

Summary

Range-bound markets are difficult for moving average strategies because they remove directional edge and introduce constant mean reversion. In these environments, it's crucial to recognize the flattening of MAs and filter out misleading signals. With the right configurations—like VWMA, envelope bands, and smoothed MAs—you can avoid whipsaws and even use flat MAs as strategic tools to trade back toward the mean. By understanding the rhythm of chop, traders can protect capital and wait for trend conditions to return.

Key Takeaways

➤ Flat or crisscrossing moving averages are early signs of a range-bound market—avoid trend-following entries during these times.

➤ Use tools like ADX and MA slope filters to confirm low-momentum environments and stand aside until direction returns.

➤ VWMA, smoothed MAs, and envelope bands are more effective than standard MAs in chop.

➤ Mean reversion strategies—like fading price extremes around a flat 20 or 50 EMA—can be more profitable than chasing breakouts.

➤ Oil, gold, and index futures all display unique choppy behaviors where MAs still provide key mean levels, especially when combined with structure and volume.

➤ Avoid overtrading. Chop offers fewer clean opportunities. Focus on protecting your capital and preparing for the next trend move.

Chapter 16

Moving Average Rejection Zones – Trading the Bounce, Not the Break

Introduction

Most traders are taught to look for breakouts or crossovers of moving averages. But often, the *most powerful opportunities* occur not when price breaks through a moving average—but when it **rejects it**.

In this chapter, we'll explore the concept of *moving average rejection zones*—areas around key MAs where price frequently bounces instead of breaking. You'll learn how to identify these zones, what types of MAs work best for rejections, and how to time entries for optimal risk-reward.

What Is a Moving Average Rejection Zone?

- **Definition**: A moving average rejection zone is a range of price action surrounding a key moving average where price frequently *tests* but fails to break through—then bounces away with momentum.
- **Purpose**: These zones are key for:
    - Trend continuation entries.
    - Low-risk pullback setups.
    - Identifying institutional support/resistance.

Why Price Rejects MAs

- **Dynamic Support/Resistance**: Institutions and algorithms often use moving averages (e.g., 20 EMA, 50 SMA, VWAP) as dynamic zones for limit orders.

- **Liquidity Pools**: Price pulls into these areas where large orders await execution. Once filled, price sharply moves away—causing the "rejection."

- **Psychological Anchors**: Many traders use MAs for stop placement or confirmation. Rejections shake out weak hands and confirm dominant trends.

Best Moving Averages for Rejection-Based Setups

- **20 EMA (Exponential Moving Average)**:
    - Responds quickly and is widely respected in intraday and swing trading.
    - Especially useful on the 5-min and 15-min charts in trending markets.

- **50 SMA (Simple Moving Average)**:
    - Offers deeper pullbacks and stronger reactions—ideal on 30-min and 1-hour charts.

- **VWAP (Volume-Weighted Average Price)**:
    - Used by institutions and day traders. Price often rejects this area during the session.

- **Anchored VWAP**:
    - Excellent for tracking rejections from specific highs, lows, or news events.

How to Define a Rejection Zone

- **Not a Fixed Price**:
    - A rejection zone isn't a single level—it's a buffer **above and below** the MA.
- **Zone Width Guidelines**:
    - For fast MAs (e.g., 9 or 20 EMA): zone = ±0.1%–0.3% of price.
    - For slower MAs (e.g., 50 or 200 SMA): zone = ±0.5%–1%.
- **Visual Confirmation**:
    - Look for multiple wicks or failed closes beyond the MA.
    - Bullish rejections: long lower wicks touching MA zone.
    - Bearish rejections: long upper wicks into MA zone.

Strategies for Trading Rejections (Not Breakouts)

- **Wait for the Reaction, Not the Touch**:
  - Let price test the zone—look for candles with rejection wicks, volume spikes, or engulfing bars.

- **Enter on Confirmation**:
  - After a rejection wick or failed break candle, enter on the break of that candle's high (bullish) or low (bearish).

- **Use Tight Stops Below the Zone**:
  - If your rejection zone is around the 20 EMA, set stops a few ticks beyond the entire buffer—not just the MA itself.

- **Confluence Increases Strength**:
  - Rejection zones are strongest when:
    - Aligned with horizontal support/resistance.

        - Occurring near Fibonacci retracements (38.2%, 61.8%).
        - In sync with higher timeframe trend direction.

Rejection Zone vs Breakout Trap

- **The Fake Break Pattern**:
    - Price closes briefly above the MA—only to reverse strongly back in the opposite direction. A hallmark of liquidity hunting.
- **Trap Signal Entry**:
    - After a false breakout, enter on the candle that engulfs or negates it.
    - These setups are ideal for scalps or reversal plays with high reward-to-risk.

Summary

Moving average rejection zones are powerful, overlooked tools for trend continuation and reversal setups. Rather than anticipating a break of a moving average, smart traders wait for price to test and reject the level—often confirming that larger market participants are defending the zone. By mastering this concept, you gain the ability to time high-conviction entries with excellent risk control, especially in fast-moving futures markets like oil, gold, and the S&P 500.

Key Takeaways

➢ A moving average rejection zone is a buffer area around an MA where price frequently bounces instead of breaking.

➢ Price often rejects MAs due to dynamic support/resistance, institutional orders, and algorithmic behavior.

➢ The 20 EMA, 50 SMA, VWAP, and Anchored VWAP are ideal for identifying these zones.

➢ Confirm rejection using candle wicks, volume patterns, and failed breakout structures.

➢ Confluence (with structure, Fibonacci, and higher timeframe trends) enhances the strength of rejection signals.

➢ Trading rejections offers tighter risk, better entries, and fewer fakeouts compared to trading breakouts.

Chapter 17

Final Summary: Mastering Moving Averages for Precision Trading

Final Summary

Throughout this book, you've built an in-depth understanding of moving averages—not just as lines on a chart, but as living, breathing indicators of market sentiment, momentum, and opportunity. From the foundational concepts of simple and exponential moving averages to advanced strategies that integrate them with other tools, you've now assembled a complete trading toolkit capable of adapting to a wide range of market conditions.

We began by stripping moving averages down to their essence—understanding how they smooth price action, reduce noise, and reveal underlying market trends. You learned how to choose the right type of moving average for your style—whether the responsiveness of an EMA suits your short-term trading or the stability of an SMA aligns with your longer-term approach. By the end of the early chapters, you had already developed the ability to see what many traders miss: that these lines are not lagging crutches, but precision instruments when understood in the right context.

As you progressed, we explored how moving averages act as dynamic support and resistance, where price action often interacts with them in predictable and profitable ways. We covered crossover strategies in detail—both the classic golden cross and death cross concepts, as well as more nuanced, high-probability crossover setups that filter out false signals. You learned not to take these signals at face value, but to confirm them with market context, volume patterns, and additional indicators to separate quality trades from noise.

We also dove into moving average envelopes, multiple time frame alignment, and the synergy of combining moving averages with oscillators, price patterns, and market timing concepts. These advanced methods transformed your understanding from simply "following the line" to using moving averages as part of a complete decision-making framework. Whether you're trading fast-moving intraday markets like oil, gold, or the S&P 500, or holding swing trades over multiple days, these strategies allow you to adapt without losing consistency.

A major takeaway was the importance of flexibility. No single moving average period or setup is perfect for all situations. Instead, the mastery comes from knowing how to adjust parameters and strategies to fit the market's volatility, the asset you're trading, and the time horizon you've chosen. By internalizing the principles behind each technique, you've gained the ability to tweak, refine, and optimize your approach in real time—something that separates skilled traders from those who rely blindly on static rules.

Equally critical was the focus on psychology and discipline. You learned that moving averages work best when paired with strong risk management, proper position sizing, and the emotional control to follow your plan even when markets test your patience. Without this mindset, even the most robust moving average strategy can be undermined by impulsive decisions. With it, you gain the mental edge that allows your system to shine over the long run.

By now, you should see moving averages not as the entire strategy, but as the backbone upon which many profitable systems can be built. They help you define trend direction, time your entries and exits, trail your stops, and stay on the right side of momentum. They work as a filter to keep you trading with the path of least resistance—maximizing your wins and minimizing the time you spend stuck in losing positions.

The real power of what you've learned lies in integration. The chapters on combining moving averages with other tools—such as RSI, volume, candlestick signals, and time-of-day analysis—showed how each element strengthens the other. In professional trading, it's rarely one indicator that gives the edge, but the way you layer confirmations until you have a setup worth risking your capital on.

From here, the path forward is simple, but not necessarily easy:

- Backtest what you've learned across different markets and conditions.
- Keep a detailed trading journal to track the performance of your moving average setups.
- Continue refining and evolving your strategies based on real-world data.
- Remain disciplined, sticking to your rules and avoiding the temptation to deviate after a few losses or wins.

Markets will change, volatility will shift, and trends will come and go—but the principles you've mastered here are timeless. Moving averages are not a magic bullet, but when used correctly, they are among the most reliable tools for navigating the chaos of price action.

As you step into your next trades, remember that mastery doesn't mean predicting every market move—it means consistently positioning yourself on the side with the highest probability of success. You now have the framework, the strategies, and the mindset to make that happen. The rest is about execution, persistence, and continuous improvement.

The markets will always reward those who are prepared, patient, and precise. You've built the skillset—now it's time to put it in motion. Trade smart, adapt quickly, and let your moving averages guide you toward precision trading success.

www.ingramcontent.com/pod-product-compliance
Lightning Source LLC
LaVergne TN
LVHW022042200926
848481LV00003B/759